BFI Modern Classics

Rob White
Series Editor

Advancing into its se...
with an established li...
to every shift in fashi...
judgments on the tru...
controversial; yet the...
going and what it car...

As part of the ...
and evaluation of cor...
influential BFI Film ...
books devote ...
critics, schola...
their chosen fi...
importance. Ins...
beautifully illustr...
matters in modern ...

Art C

Pa

Titanic

David M. Lubin

 Publishing

First published in 1999 by the
British Film Institute
21 Stephen Street, London W1P 2LN

Copyright © David M. Lubin 1999

The British Film Institute promotes greater
understanding and appreciation of, and
access to, film and moving image culture in
the UK

Series design by Andrew Barron &
Collis Clements Associates

Typeset in Italian Garamond and Swiss 721BT
by D R Bungay Associates, Burghfield, Berks

Printed in Great Britain by
Norwich Colour Print, Drayton, Norfolk

British Library Cataloguing-in-Publication Data
A catalogue record for this book is available
from the British Library
ISBN 0-85170-760-2

Contents

Titanic

Who's Seen It, Why?

For a movie that sold more tickets in its first year of release than any other motion picture in history, a movie that was the first ever to gross one billion dollars in worldwide sales, *Titanic* has been seen by few people I know. When I began telling my friends, colleagues and students that I was writing a detailed analysis of the blockbuster, I was surprised at how few of them had seen it – or at least were willing to admit they had. Eventually this response proved so predictable that I eventually switched gears – or, to use a metaphor from the film – reversed engines and now have come to be surprised when someone I know actually says, 'Oh, yes, I've seen that film.' The greatest surprise of all is when he or she adds, 'And I loved it.'

As the French sociologist Pierre Bourdieu details in *Distinction*, the consumption or non-consumption of popular culture artefacts is a means by which individuals in a society define for themselves and others their social position, their status.[1] To consume an artefact that most everyone else in your peer group has been consuming, and to relish it along with them, is to strengthen your affiliation. To make a choice *not* to consume an artefact that you perceive to be distasteful to your own class faction is likewise a means of affirming your legitimate place within that faction. Consuming or not consuming the artefact in question can even be a tactic for dissociating yourself from your present peer group in order to associate yourself with another.

Something of this sort goes on all the time as we make decisions, first, what movies to see or not see and, second, whether to be enthralled by them or instead turn up our noses and loudly protest having wasted our time. I think it has something to do with why so few of my acquaintances in the professional managerial middle class made a point of viewing *Titanic* and why, in fact, so many of them made it a point of pride to stay away from a film that was hyped almost beyond belief in the first months of its release. Refusing to see *Titanic*, or, if seeing it, refusing to be taken in by it (in a key phrase from the film dialogue, 'to let it in'), became a way of asserting one's

independence from all the journalistic gush surrounding James Cameron's
film and all the highly suspect emotional manipulation within it.

This is not to say that critics of *Titanic* are unjustified in finding it a
crude, tawdry, manipulative example of cinematic art. There are, indeed,
sound aesthetic reasons for considering the film closer in kinship and
kitsch to *Ship of Fools*, *The Poseidon Adventure* and even *The Love Boat*
than to *Battleship Potempkin*. But, still, the critical backlash against *Titanic*
in some of the popular and trade press was so excessive that one can only
wonder if the bombardment against Cameron's 'ship of dreams' wasn't
really aimed at a larger target than the particular film in question.

Leading the onslaught was the influential senior film reviewer for
the *Los Angeles Times*, Kenneth Turan, who availed himself of every
opportunity to pepper *Titanic* with grapeshot from the moment of its US
première in late December 1997 to its film-industry apotheosis the
following March when at the Academy Awards ceremony it tied the
illustrious record set in 1959 by *Ben-Hur* for the most Oscars (11) ever

won by a single film.[2] When irate readers defended *Titanic* from Turan's ridicule by proclaiming that 'proof [of the film's capacity for moving viewers] is in the box-office', Turan replied, 'Film critics, general opinion notwithstanding, are not intended to be applause meters. After all, restaurant critics don't send [consumers] straight to McDonald's on the "everybody goes there, it must be the best" theory.' Quite to the contrary, the role of critics 'must be to point out the existence and importance of other criteria for judgment besides popularity'.[3]

The enemy here appears to be contemporary popular taste, mass culture, the McDonaldization of sensibility with regard to hamburgers and blockbusters alike. Not that Turan assigns the blame for this degradation of standards to the masses themselves, but rather to the culture industry that has seduced or otherwise commandeered their attention: '*Titanic*'s ability to attract a crowd,' he continues, 'shows how desperate the mainstream audience – alienated by studio reliance on the kind of mindless violence that can be counted on to sell overseas – has become for anything even resembling old-fashioned entertainment. ... Deadened by exposure to nonstop trash ... audiences have been sadly eager to embrace a film that, putting the best face on it, is a witless counterfeit of Hollywood's Golden Age, a compendium of clichés that add up to a reasonable facsimile of a film.'

Film studies professor José Arroyo concurs not only with Turan's assessment of *Titanic*'s flaws but his conviction that these flaws are endemic to the current state of market-driven film-making: 'It is because of its lack of story-telling skills and its execrable character delineation that *Titanic* is emblematic of contemporary Hollywood action / spectacle – it is also because of this that it is not a good film.'[4] Critic Laura Miller is less measured in tone: 'That everything about *Titanic* – from its stereotyped characters to its bright, even lighting – feels ersatz and obvious may only trouble the kind of people who dislike the immaculate, synthetic recreations of real places in Disney theme parks.' Alas, most people are not Disney-proof: 'The movie works as a simple-minded entertainment that provides a setting for spectacular visual effects, and many audiences will find it adequately enjoyable,' Miller concedes with a sigh.[5]

Adequately enjoyable? Is that all? As is by now well known, audiences across the planet found *Titanic* something more than merely adequate in the pleasure – and, indeed, pain – it stimulated. In an effort to make sense of the film's staggeringly unexpected audience appeal, a *Newsweek* story in February 1998 told of an 18-year-old US college student named Gina Latta who wears blue nail polish, has her ears triple pierced, favours David Lynch movies, and even regards the dialogue in *Titanic* as 'incredibly cheesy'. Nonetheless, in the two months since the film's US première, Latta had seen it four times: 'The first time I saw it, I got out of the theater and I was having a cigarette with a friend and we couldn't stop crying. I was so overwhelmed at how sad it was.'[6]

The *Newsweek* piece drew upon a variety of media producers and pundits to suggest that the movie was tapping into widespread public desires to move beyond, in Camille Paglia's words, 'shallow post-modernist irony and cynicism' toward a cynicism-free product that celebrates themes of selflessness, self-sacrifice and cross-class bonding. Feminist author Mary Pipher (*Reviving Orphelia*) contended that the movie was 'really about [Jack] helping [Rose] become an authentic whole person', while 29-year-old male Japanese magazine editor Naoshi Kayashima valued it as an examination of male cowardice and courage ('a movie about how men choose their endings'), and 63-year-old theatre director André Gregory explained that, for him, 'the movie was really about that old woman. I was moved that she could fight her way out of a life that was imposed on her by her family, and by society.'[7]

The thrust of the *Newsweek* coverage was to designate *Titanic* as a women's film with crossover appeal to men who want more from a movie than simply colossal effects and brutal physical action. Yet despite *Newsweek*'s acknowledgment of the film's emotional appeal to male as well as female filmgoers, it characterized *Titanic*'s typical viewer – particularly its repeat viewer – as a female under the age of 25. Polls cited by the article found that 60 per cent of *Titanic*'s audiences were female, 63 per cent of its viewers were under 25, and 45 per cent of all women under 25 who had seen the movie had seen it at least twice. No surprise then that press accounts of the movie's unprecedented box-office success took it upon themselves to explain it as the revenge of the 'chick flick' against the more typical 'dick flick' that Cameron and other high-testosterone action directors had previously turned into box-office megahits. A cartoon in *Time* drolly advanced this point of view by depicting a city block with two queues of consumers: the all-female queue stands in front of a cinema with the name *Titanic* blazoned across its marquee; the all-male queue lines up before a pharmacy with a sign in the window announcing 'Viagra Now Available'.[8]

Throughout the spring of 1998, reports of *Titanic* hysteria seemed determined to resurrect the old cultural stereotype of tear-streaked, weak-kneed female idolators constitutionally incapable of withstanding the obsessive impulses programmed into them by the merchants of shlock. Elvis, the early Beatles, and now *Titanic*. In March the Associated Press carried an item about a 12-year-old Italian girl who had devotedly attended the movie every single day since December. In May the teen magazine *Sugar* told of a 14-year-old English girl and her mum who had

The commerce of sexual politics. © Jack Ziegler from cartoonbank.com. All rights reserved

sat through a total of 84 screenings of the epic since its UK release at the end of January.[9] In June an Associated Press news brief reported that an unidentified Norwegian woman, mid- to late thirties in age, had plunged to her death from the bow railing of a Scandinavian cruise ship, where she had positioned herself at sunset in imitation of Rose's 'flying' scene. A rash of similar, if non-fatal, incidents on other cruise ships in other seas led transportation safety boards to issue stern warnings that passengers must not be permitted to climb onto ship railings.[10]

It's my contention, though, that the appeal of Cameron's film extends well beyond female moviegoers looking for a good cry, stolid males hoping to provide a manly shoulder to cry on, and untold legions of 'Titaniacs' who have long constituted a guaranteed audience for any movie or book (possibly even this book) that takes the doomed ocean liner as its topic. What the following analysis suggests is that *Titanic* offers its audiences a way to *think about* relevant modern issues of culture and class. While not by any means an intellectual film (and far less an intellectual's film), *Titanic* nevertheless prompts viewers to pose to themselves questions about our society's divide between rich and poor, the nature of love, the meaning of sacrifice, and modernity's faith in, even obsession with, technological prowess and mastery over nature.

Indeed, these same questions were raised in the minds of the general public from the very first reports of *Titanic*'s collision with the iceberg on the night of 14 April 1912.[11] In the immediate aftermath of the sinking, Joseph Conrad used it as an occasion to blame the steamship lines for fetishizing size, speed and profits, while Thomas Hardy, in a poem penned for a memorial service one month after the disaster, expressed anew his naturalist creed that fate rules human destiny and, in this instance, ordained for the great ship and the even greater iceberg an unavoidable 'Convergence of the Twain'.[12] On Sunday, 21 April 1912, the prominent New York Presbyterian minister Charles H. Parkurst declared the sinking a 'terrific and ghastly illustration of what things come to when men throw God out at the door', while in Washington, DC, on the same Sunday the Archbishop of Baltimore announced that 'the remote cause of this unspeakable disaster is the excessive pursuit of luxury'. To a

Universalist minister in Indianapolis, 'The underlying cause of it all is our social allegiance to the twin gods of Mammon, *speed* and *greed*.'[13]

But it wasn't only the high and mighty who strove to decipher the deeper meanings of the catastrophe. Advocates for women's rights saw the sinking as a warning of what happens to society when male hubris goes unchecked by female influence (women, supposedly, would have ensured there were enough lifeboats on board), whereas their opponents, many of them women themselves, believed that the much-touted rescue of women and children testified, if not to male superiority, then at least to male nobility and selflessness. 'Let the suffragists remember this,' advised the author of a letter to the *Baltimore Sun*. 'When the Lord created woman and placed her under the protection of man he had her well provided for. The Titanic disaster proves it very plainly.'[14] The radical labour agitator

The search for meaning begins (Cultural Services, Southampton City Council)

Mother Jones found arguments of this sort nauseating, particularly when it was the men in first class who were being extolled. In a speech to striking coal miners she remarked, 'The papers came out and said those millionaires tried to save the women. Oh, Lord, why don't they give up their millions if they want to save the women and children? Why do they rob them of home, why do they rob millions of women to fill the hell-holes of capitalism?'[15]

Similarly, the socialist *Jewish Daily Forward* imagined drowned steerage passengers bemoaning the praise given by the mainstream press to the swells in first class:

Oy, that aristocrat fought to get into a boat but was held back by pistols. Now the papers are filled with their heroism. We poor folk who died while stoking the fires in the engine room until the very last minute, we third-class passengers who truly showed heroism, about us they write nothing.

In 1912, Delta blues musician Leadbelly pictured his fellow African-American, world heavyweight boxing champion Jack Johnson, dancing with joy at the news of the sinking: 'Jack Johnson want to get on board / Captain he said, "I ain't haulin' no coal," / Fare thee, Titanic, fare thee well. / When he heard about that mighty shock, / You mighta seen a man doin' the Eagle Rock.'[16]

The film *Titanic* produces social meanings out of the crash no less so than did the original *Titanic* news reports, sermons, speeches and songs. Like most of these earlier accounts, Cameron's movie is heavy-handed and partisan and, like many of them, it is also populist (though much less so than, say, the speech by Mother Jones). From first to last, it tells the story explicitly in terms of class and gender (but not, like Leadbelly, in terms of race). Unquestionably an ideological film, it proclaims to its viewers in all sorts of ways that intuitive knowledge surpasses instrumental rationality, that greed is bad, elitism wrong, freedom a virtue, self-sacrifice noble, and, above all, that true love transcends death. These and other old-fashioned (or out-of-fashion) meanings dramatically and spectacularly put forth by the film are, in essence, the basis of its worldwide success.

Framing History

The movie opens with yellowed and slightly out-of-focus 'old-time' footage of the *Titanic* harboured in Southampton, England, on the historic morning of its departure in April 1912.[17] Crowds of passengers, porters, farewell-bidders and sightseers throng the pier and the decks of the ship. What we see is not actual historical footage but an expertly crafted fabrication of such.

A shot of a man operating an old-time, hand-cranked movie camera suggests that the footage we are viewing was filmed on-site by cameras of a similar vintage. Shots from various angles are gracefully dissolved one into

another, and over it all a synthesized bagpipe and a high-pitched female voice emit a wordless, plaintive, Gaelic lament.

Hence, from the outset of the film, a handful of contrasting and complementary signifiers, all related to the representation of history, are blended together. We see crowds, which tell us we are in the objective realm of the public sphere, mass society, modern history. We see footage shot in the rough and jerky newsreel style that has long been associated with the on-site recording of historical events as they occur. The yellow tint of the footage suggests that it is genuinely old – indeed, contemporaneous with the occasion in question – and therefore authentic in its documentation. The leisurely dissolves from one camera position to

The making of history-in-the-making

another invoke the cinematic language of memory and distance from the past (whereas abrupt cuts normally suggest directness, immediacy, the present). Finally, the plangent Gaelic rhythms and archaic-sounding lament register as signifiers of the oral tradition, folklore, the age-old keening of women for loved ones lost to the sea.

These first moments of busy and bustling history-in-the-making dissolve into a medium shot of midnight blue ocean waters rolling and swelling in a timeless, ahistorical rhythm. The ethereal singing continues. Cut to underwater, a ponderous darkness illuminated by travelling points of light that approach from the distance and glide eerily toward the lower foreground like alien spaceships in a science-fiction film. The lights, we quickly learn, belong to a pair of submersibles exploring the wreckage of the *Titanic* in time-present.

The conjunction of nature and history; Close Encounters under the sea

Thus, in the first three minutes of the three-and-a-quarter hour film, the three-act historical trajectory of the ship is delineated: it was launched, it was lost at sea, it was found. This sequence also happens to define the dramatic trajectory of the film's love affair: it is launched (the lovers meet and fall in love), it is lost (they struggle with the ocean and the man succumbs), it is recovered (the woman rejoins her lost love in the memory or fantasy or transmission-to-death that concludes the story).

The paralleling of these two trajectories – ship and love affair – is the primary structural device of the film. It also embodies the film's theory of history: the past can only be truly known when seen through the eyes and heard through the ears of one who actually lived it.

Such is the governing premise of oral history. It is also a central tenet of the New Social History, a movement among historians that since the 1960s has urged that the past be investigated not from 'the top down' (concentrating on the rich and mighty, usually men) but from 'the bottom up' (attending to the oppressed, the underclassed, and the previously silenced, including women of any social class). The central narrative of *Titanic* thus models itself on the New Social History, for while it provides glimpses of influential and well-documented historical figures, such as Captain E. J. Smith, ship designer Thomas Andrews, chairman of the White Star shipping lines, J. Bruce Ismay, and the industrialists John Jacob Astor and Benjamin Guggenheim, it focuses instead on the experiences of (fictitious) 'ordinary' people: the young middle-class woman, Rose DeWitt Bukater, and her bohemian artist lover, Jack Dawson, and, to a much lesser extent, his paradigmatic immigrant comrades, Fabrizio de Rossi and Tommy Ryan.

Titanic, this is to say, presents itself to its audiences with the accoutrements of oral history and upstairs-downstairs social history. All narratives – historical, literary or otherwise – rely on self-authenticating devices, be they scholarly footnotes or authorial direct address ('Believe this, dear Reader, for what I am about to tell is true'). *Titanic* relies on the rhetorical modes and conventions of oral and social history as they have filtered through to the general public over the past two to three decades. It wraps itself in this populist discourse of authenticity in order to heighten its audience's willingness, indeed, eagerness, to suspend disbelief.

Aboard the submersible a different regime of truth holds sway. Here is the domain of scientific technology, with blinking lights, sonar bleeps, computers, LED displays, video monitors and a remote-operated camera. All of these, we quickly sense, are being activated for the gathering, measurement, quantification and analysis of underwater data. The viewer is suddenly confronted with an impersonal numerical realm, far indeed from the world of living bodies, personal relationships and age-old grief already summoned forth by the opening moments. The first spoken line of the film invokes the quantitative perspective: 'Thirteen meters. You should see it.'

With this we first glimpse the skeletal wreckage of *Titanic*. Not all of it, but rather the bow of the ship and, most notably, the railing. Only later does the irony of this moment become apparent, for it is at this railing that Jack will whoop with joy, 'I'm the king of the world!' and here again still

Jack's space

later that Rose will rapturously spread her arms like a great bird soaring through the universe.

The commander of the sub, Brock Lovett, a handsome, light-haired, scruffy young man who sports a gold earring (signifier of late 1990s hipness), points a handheld video-recorder out the porthole while solemnly narrating the moment at hand, presumably for a TV documentary in the works: 'Seeing her [the wreckage] coming out of the darkness, like a ghost ship, still gets me every time. To see the sad ruin of the great ship sitting here, where she landed … after her long fall from the world above.' The final moments of *Titanic* will pull out all stops in order to make Lovett's an accurate description of the viewer's emotional experience. But those moments lie three hours in the future. For now, his remark sounds forced and hollow. An assistant snorts, 'You're so full of shit, boss.' Lovett snaps off the video-recorder and grins.

The voice that utters the comment belongs to the submersible's operator, Lewis Bodine. A minor character, Lewis nonetheless plays a crucial role in *Titanic*, for he is the representative figure of technological modernity that it is the burden of the film to soften and humanize. Lewis is fat and unkempt, a young ponytailed techno-geek possessed of a beer gut, wire-rim glasses and (as revealed at various intervals through the film) an array of T-shirts, the most memorable of which depicts a bright yellow smiley face splattered with blood from a bullet-hole to its brain. In effect, Lewis will play antagonist to the frame story's protagonist, the 1990s Rose. He is the one who is least prepared to accept her claim that she is the same Rose Bukater who is thought to have died in the sinking. 'She's a god-damned liar, some nutcase seeking money or publicity,' he warns Brock. 'Like that Russian babe, Anaesthesia.'

His malapropism amounts to more than a gag. Anaesthesia, of course, is the loss of physical sensation brought about by disease or an anaesthetic. Lewis is the film's personification of modern emotional anaesthesia, for what do all his technological gadgets and flippant remarks amount to if not a means of filtering out or otherwise disavowing memory, frailty and pain? What the film itself will attempt to accomplish is the restoration of pain and memory, for it will seek to make us feel and know what it must have been like to be aboard the *Titanic* the night that it sank. The crucial claim the film makes is that the act of dramatizing the past in its full emotional spectrum, through the use of fictional characters and fictitious situations, honours that past in a manner superior to what can be achieved by strictly technological and documentary means of gathering and investigating historical data.

Lewis manoeuvres a remote-operated camera ('ROV') onto and into the *Titanic* wreckage. With a point-of-view shot through its lens, we float along an exterior passageway into the ship itself. This is a critical shot that will be reprised in the final moments of the film with enormous psychological resonance. But for now it works in a straightforward fashion

to draw us aboard and into the mysterious ghost vessel. Lewis, shown in cutaway with a 'Snoop Vision' visor on his head and his tongue hanging from his mouth, makes crude, quasi-sexual comments like, 'We're in, baby, we're there!' and 'Oh, baby, baby! Are you seeing this, boss?' When the camera passes a commode at the bottom of the sea, he quips, 'Oops, someone left the water running.'

In contrast to this prosaic video footage made by the ROV is film-making of an entirely different order, showing us with a series of poetically lit close-ups of personal effects half buried in the sand what the robot camera misses: a lady's boot, a pair of glasses, the white moon face of a child's porcelain doll. Each of these monumental close-ups is separated from the others by a fade-out / fade-in combination, which in the syntax of

In search of underwater treasure

cinema gives them each a phenomenological magnificence and tragic isolation. No crude voice-over here; this is a private and numinous world that Lewis's 'Snoop Vision' cannot fathom.

The ROV locates an iron safe in a watery state room. 'It's payday, boys!' Brock exclaims. When the safe is brought aboard the salvage ship and blasted open, rusty orange mud oozes out. Brock reaches in and pulls out a leather portfolio, but the disappointment on his face indicates that whatever he was expecting to find is not there. This absence introduces us to what is being sought, 'the Heart of the Ocean', a legendary jewel (according to the fiction of the story) that once belonged to Louis XVI, disappeared during the French Revolution, and never surfaced again until 1912, when Cal Hockley, son of a Pittsburgh steel magnate, purchased it as a wedding gift for his fiancée, Rose DeWitt Bukater. The Heart of the Ocean thus functions as the plot pretext – what Hitchcock liked to call the 'MacGuffin' – providing motivation for Brock to bring Rose to the salvage site and ask her to tell her story.[18]

The Heart of the Ocean is more than merely a MacGuffin, however. In its slipperiness as a signifier, it operates like the earrings in Max Ophuls's *The Earrings of Madame de …* (1953), in which jewels that initially hold only pecuniary interest accrete additional layers of meaning as they pass in a happenstance manner from one owner to another. In *Titanic*, the Heart of the Ocean is at first equated with venality ('It's payday!'), corruption (the court of Louis XVI), social upheaval (the French Revolution), and anti-democratic elitism ('We are royalty, Rose,' Cal haughtily informs his fiancée).

Rose comes to see that for Cal the necklace, like Rose herself, is an object of conspicuous consumption, a means of publicly displaying his power and wealth. She later asks Jack to draw her wearing nothing but the diamond, and then she returns the drawing and the diamond to Cal's strongbox with the note, 'Darling, now you can keep us both locked in your safe.' The diamond subsequently passes to Cal's solemn and ironically named valet, Lovejoy (he appears neither loving nor joyful), who plants it on Jack as incriminating evidence. It passes back to the safe, then to Cal, and finally, inadvertently, to Rose. At the very end of the film it will

pass to the ocean itself, flung by Rose into the depths of the sea, where it can now forever be free of its former pecuniary status.[19]

     When we first see Rose, who is sitting at a potter's wheel in an airy, plant-filled studio perched over the Pacific Ocean, she is wearing earrings shaped like the Heart of the Ocean (as seen in the drawing recovered from the safe), and the clay that oozes between her fingers is identical in colour

The Earrings of Madame de …; the Heart of the Ocean

and texture to the mud that oozed from the safe when Brock opened it. Thus, our first glimpse of Rose identifies her metonymically with the Heart of the Ocean (her replica earrings), the ocean itself (the view from her window), the bottom of the sea (the orange mud between her fingers), organic life (the plants) and artistic creativity (Jack's drawing, her pottery).[20]

Accompanied by her granddaughter Lizzy, an attractive, outdoorsy sort of blonde, and an array of framed photographs (the significance of which will be clarified in the final moments of the film), Rose is transported to the salvage ship somewhere in the midst of the North Atlantic and urged to account for the whereabouts of the missing diamond. It is at this moment, when she descends from the helicopter that has brought her aboard, that she first comes into contrast with Lewis, the slovenly and sceptical computer geek wearing the blood-splattered smiley face.

When Lewis shows Rose – and, most helpfully for comprehension of later sequences, the film audience – a computer-generated step-by-step recreation of the *Titanic*'s collision with the iceberg and its plunge to the ocean floor, Rose replies with ironic understatement, 'Thank you for that fine forensic analysis, Mr Bodine. Of course the experience of it was

somewhat different.' The movie we are about to see aims to provide 'the experience of it' through the artifice of cinematic story-telling. To invoke the title of Cameron's previous film, *Titanic* will provide 'true lies' about the past in order to bring us closer to that remote era than mere facts, documents and salvaged artefacts ever could.

A forensic analysis

Thousands of feet above the wreckage of the once magnificent ocean liner, Rose begins her account of *Titanic*'s – and her own – maiden voyage. By the end of the narration, some three hours hence, she will have won everyone over to her side, including Lewis, whose face will be marked by a tear. Brock, speaking to Rose's granddaughter, will hold up that classic signifier of masculine prowess, a cigar, that he has been saving for the triumph and remuneration of discovering the Heart of the Ocean. As he flings it into the sea, he will explain: 'Three years, I've thought of nothing but *Titanic*. But I never got it. I never let it in.' What he never let in was the personal side of the disaster, the human dimension, that the film itself, with Rose as its mouthpiece, strives to depict. (Brock, surely, is a stand-in for James Cameron, who took three years to make the film, but presumably Cameron feels that he, unlike his alter ego, 'got' the personal dimension – and also unlike Brock, as it turns out, ultimately recouped his investment.)

'It's been 84 years,' she begins. 'And I can still smell the fresh paint. The china had never been used. The sheets had never been slept in…. *Titanic* was called the ship of dreams. And it was – it really was.' Here the eerie, high-pitched singing returns, and with it the identical newsreel-like images that were shown at the start of the film, only now they are vividly coloured, not tinged with yellow, and they are in sharp focus rather than soft. By repeating these introductory shots of leave-taking, the film plays a cunning trick, for if the images in the aged Rose's head are the same as those first images shown, albeit even brighter and sharper, the accuracy of her recollection of that distant day is confirmed. A similar effect occurs in Orson Welles's 1941 fictional biopic, *Citizen Kane*: later events in the narrative acquire credibility – and often irony, as well – because of the way they line up with earlier representations of those same events in the faux newsreel documentary that begins the film. In both cases, a sleight-of-hand has taken place, since the 'historical' footage is itself fiction doctored up to look like fact.

Structurally, the extended prologue of *Titanic* ends with the bravura sequence that introduces the teenage Rose DeWitt Bukater on the morning that she boards the *Titanic*. A series of detail shots of a young woman exiting from a chauffeur-driven motor car – a gloved hand, the brim of an enormous purple hat – give way to an overhead shot, the camera swanning down from a lofty angle toward that ostentatious hat at the very moment that Rose lifts her head to view the mighty ocean liner and, in so doing, first reveals herself to our gaze. This is a shot of great dramatic flourish, similar to John Ford's famous track-in on John Wayne as the Ringo Kid in *Stagecoach* (1939). It's hyperbolic, egotistical and visceral, and in that way perfectly suited to the consciousness and emotional state, not of the calm, clear-sighted 101-year-old woman who tells the story, but rather the emotional 17-year-old who is her romantic protagonist.

Young Rose is to be understood as a representative of modernity. She is the modern woman who was much in the news at the time of the

The two Roses

great liner's 'maiden' voyage: bold, headstrong, determined, dissatisfied with the subservient role accorded her by patriarchal tradition. In the UK suffragettes (or suffragists, as their counterparts were called in the US) campaigned for the right to vote in general elections and to own property directly rather than through the proxy of their husbands. Rose is not depicted as having a suffragist consciousness, but rather what might be thought of as a suffragist pre-consciousness. Says the present Rose in voice-over as we gaze at the adolescent Rose against the backdrop of the *Titanic*: 'It was the ship of dreams to everyone else. To me it was a slave ship – taking me back to America in chains. Outwardly, I was everything a well-brought up young lady should be. Inside I was screaming.'

She boards the *Titanic* chafing at her fiancé's domineering ways, but because she has as yet no way of articulating her rage and releasing herself from the dreadfulness of an arranged marriage, she will soon attempt suicide. By the conclusion of the film, however, we are meant to see that Rose came away from the *Titanic* disaster a changed person, capable of embracing life to the fullest, as represented by the photo gallery at her bedside table: Rose as aviatrix, Rose as Hemingwayesque deep-sea angler, Rose on horseback in the surf.

She is to be understood, that is, as the personification of the twentieth-century female, starting off the century as a suppressed and timid girl but becoming, through crisis and struggle, an expressive, mature

The modern woman

and self-actualized woman. The transformation of identity that we are to witness is hinted at by the recovered object that Rose caresses in her hand, an art-nouveau hair comb shaped like a butterfly.

The American Adam

The next section of *Titanic* introduces Jack Dawson, the youth who will promptly become young Rose's love interest. Jack is a stock character – a free spirit, a bohemian, a proto-hippie – and as such he undergoes no character development over the course of the film. But though he himself does not significantly change, he is the narrative agent of change or, in technical terms, the story catalyst. His role in the film is to awaken in Rose the strength and self-knowledge needed for her to liberate herself from her class- and gender-based chains.

Says Jack when we first meet him: 'Moment of truth. Somebody's life is about to change.' These words are telling, of course; the character unknowingly predicting what is about to occur to him, Rose and, indeed, the 2,200 other passengers and crew on the *Titanic*. His invocation of truth also resurrects the assertion already put in place that fiction's 'lies' can actually be more truthful than the facts provided by non-fiction. But the immediate reference is neither to the narrative ahead nor to the frame story behind, but rather to the poker game in which he is presently involved. Jack is playing cards in a dockside shanty with his Italian friend Fabrizio and other transients, and has wagered all that he owns (not much) against a pair of third-class tickets to America. The current owners of the tickets are two young Swedes, Sven and Olaf. When one of these two realizes that Jack has won their passage to America, he hauls off as though to slug Jack in the face, but at the last moment delivers a haymaker to his compatriot.

The moment is played for laughs – Jack even screws up his face, waiting for the blow that does not come. We're in the clearly recognizable territory here of the Saturday morning cowboy film, though the setting is a pub in Southampton, England, rather than a saloon in Buzzard Gulch. But lying even further behind the six-gun serial as a referent is 'The Blue Hotel' (1899), Stephen Crane's oft-anthologized short story about a frontier card game. In the story, one of the players, a Swede, loses first the game, then his temper, and then finally his life, having provoked another man into killing him.

Crane's *fin-de-siècle* fatalism attests to a theory of self-determination, but not in the positive sense espoused by Emerson in his prose essays written in the expansive years before the Civil War. Instead, self-determination in Crane's world means that sooner or later every individual is bound to fulfil the self-destructive impulses that are lodged within. Such is anything but the theory of self-determination underlying *Titanic*, for Jack Dawson is held up by the film as a model and apostle of optimistic Emersonian self-reliance. Self-determination is the message he conveys to Rose over and over and over again: 'You can do it, Rose. … I trust you. … You have the strength,' and so forth. Whereas the hapless antiheroes of Crane's naturalist fiction are done in by their foibles or only manage to survive by dumb luck, the hero and heroine of *Titanic* manage to create their own reality amid universal panic and thus transcend the crushing inexorability of fate.

Thus Jack *wins* his ticket of passage (as opposed simply to having been given it), he *runs* to catch the ship as it is about to pull away from the dock, he *talks* his way aboard (bypassing a required medical inspection), he *rescues* Rose from her suicide attempt (rather than passively observing a distraught girl hasten by while he reclines in reverie on a bench). At the end, when he is freezing to death in the water, he can say, 'Winning that ticket was the best thing that ever happened to me,' because, in the terms of the Victorian parlour-favourite poem 'Invictus', he has been the master of his fate and the captain of his soul from first to last. He may die in the end, but only because he has chosen to dog-paddle in the freezing water alongside Rose on her makeshift raft rather than tip her off and climb onto it himself, as might a figure in a naturalist novel. One of the characters in 'The Blue Hotel' remarks that the poor devil goaded by the Swede into killing him 'isn't even a noun. He is a kind of adverb.'[21] Jack Dawson, on the other hand, is verb, all verb.

The name 'Jack Dawson', in fact, alludes to the American writer of the *Titanic* era most internationally admired as an active verb, Jack London. Like Jack Dawson, Jack London was an orphan – actually, an illegitimate child whose mother all but abandoned him – who worked shrimp boats off the Monterey coast and rode horses in the surf. As a youth London was also a gang member, a pirate, a socialist and a hobo who did time in jail before heading up to the Alaskan Yukon (its capital, Dawson City) to take part in the Klondike gold rush. It was this latter experience that provided him with the source material for his first worldwide best-seller, *The Call of the Wild* (1903).

In his zeal for fresh experience and with his knack for quick-witted improvisation, Jack Dawson is indeed a boy's adventure idealization of Jack London, possessing none of the ravaging insecurity, self-loathing and alcoholic destructiveness that London confessed about himself in his autobiography. Nor does *Titanic* subscribe to London's popularized version

of turn-of-the-century naturalism, which, like Crane's, held that individuals are ultimately prisoners of their environment and heredity. *Titanic*, too, has its base and selfish figures (the capitalist Cal Hockley, his man-servant Lovejoy, and White Star executive Bruce Ismay) and its metaphoric embodiments of nature's indifference to human well-being (the iceberg, the ocean). But thematically these dire instances are more than offset not only by Jack's gallant selflessness and Rose's acquisition of self-reliance, but also by the kindly interventions of minor characters such as Molly Brown, Mr Andrews and Second Officer Lightoller, as well as by the luminous self-effacement of the band and by Benjamin Guggenheim's astonishing poise in the face of death. *Titanic*, this is to say, gives us London without the *fin-de-siècle* pessimism and socialist venom: London Lite. Its Jack Dawson is

Jack as active verb

nothing more nor less than the stout-hearted, self-assured and romantically chivalrous vagabond artist that many of London's admirers, then and now, incorrectly imagine him to have been.

In that exuberant moment when Jack leans over the bow of the ship and thrills to the silver dolphins racing ahead, he is an American Adam surveying the animals of Eden, an Emersonian eyeball revelling in the unmatched splendours of nature. When he raises his arms toward the infinitude of the oncoming West and whoops 'I'm the king of the world!' it's a moment that Cooper and Mark Twain and Emerson and Whitman and the romantic American landscape painter Thomas Cole would have applauded as the rightful response of the American democrat to the pristine glories of the New World (though surely they would have questioned the use of the monarchical term). When, in the next sequence at that railing, Rose exclaims, 'Why can't I be like you, Jack? Just head out for the horizon whenever I feel like it,' she voices the awe, if not wishful thinking, that society-bound readers and moviegoers throughout the world have for generations felt about mythic American heroes from Daniel Boone and Natty Bumppo to Hollywood's Shane and the Ringo Kid.[22]

Ships and Dancers Stretch Their Legs

Jack flies with Fabrizio through the crowds at dockside and onto the ship as it is to pull away. Running down a corridor, he cries with glee, and not a little dramatic irony, 'We are the luckiest sons of bitches in the world!' The pace of the film picks up, the music soars, the ship departs.

The enormity of the *Titanic*

The ship, the captain, the workers

A shot of the bow of the liner slicing through the harbour waters while being observed at point-blank range by a lone figure on a small sailboat jolts the viewer with a sudden recognition of the ship's enormity. Earlier in the film we had heard talk of its scale, but now for the first time we *see* it.

The captain orders his chief officer, 'Take it to sea, Mr Murdoch. Let's stretch her legs.' For the first time we glimpse the bowels of the ship. The gleaming pipes, pulleys and pistons mesh together in a synchronized rhythm suggesting the well-oiled muscularity of a thoroughbred. Cinematically, the industrial interiors envisioned by Fritz Lang's *Metropolis* (1926) and Charlie Chaplin's *Modern Times* (1936) are invoked, but whereas in those films industrial mechanization possessed an oppressive or even diabolic aura, here high mechanization provides an awe-inspiring spectacle of cathedralesque proportions. From lowest deck to top, the actual *Titanic* was as tall as an eleven-story building, and its four huge funnels reached half as high again. An advertising diagram used by the White Star Line up-ended the vessel (actually, its sister ship the *Olympic*) and placed it in a line-up with other remarkable architectural accomplishments of history to show that at 882 feet (229 meters) its height exceeded those of the Great Pyramid, Cologne Cathedral, the Washington Monument and, what was then the tallest building in the world and a symbol of modern engineering prowess, the Woolworth Building in New York. At the time of its launching, the *Titanic* was the epitome of industrial and commercial modernity.

There is a cutaway to the propeller blades deep in the water as they gather speed. Cameron now unleashes the first of the great aerial travelling shots that, together with the pumped-up, *Chariots of Fire*-style synthesizer music, adore the mighty vessel as it takes command of the sea. There's a double kick here. We are asked to admire not only the incredible technological (and financial) achievement of the shipbuilders of 1912 who put this vessel in the water, but also that of the 1997 film-makers who launched its re-creation. Any viewer of today reasonably aware of computer-generated cinematic imagery might well take note during this spectacular shot that real-life actors are being conjoined with a scale-model ship and digital animation figures in order to create the illusion of a genuine passenger ship plunging ahead into an actual sea. Nonetheless, the sensation of size, power and magnitude, and of history having been convincingly re-created, is momentarily overwhelming.

Cinematic special effects, such as the one employed in this and later shots of the *Titanic* as it cuts through the sea or sinks into it, are meant to re-create reality but to do so with such an extravagance of detail as to stun the viewer with the excellence of the simulacrum. Illusionism of this sort goes back millennia before the era of Georges Méliès, the cinema's first maestro of special effects. Pliny tells of the ancient artist Zeuxis, whose still-life painting of a basket of fruit was so deceivingly real that crows swept down from the sky in a misguided effort to make off with the grapes. Closer to the era of cinema, nineteenth-century American viewers gasped at and applauded the amazing visual trickery of trompe l'oeil specialists such as William Harnett and John Haberle, who, through a magical application of paint on canvas, re-created the artefacts of daily life with astonishing verisimilitude.

Spectators also lined up for the privilege of standing aghast before oversized landscape paintings by artists such as Frederic Church, whose far-ranging panoramas were built upon a scaffolding of myriad details. Church's celebrated *Heart of the Andes* (1859), at the time the highest-

Frederic Edwin Church, *The Icebergs* (Dallas Museum of Art)

priced painting ever sold by a living American, was theatrically framed by curtains, and admirers examined it through opera glasses to marvel better at its infinite array of minute details and soaring vistas. His large-scale, proto-cinematic paintings *Niagara* (1857) and *Icebergs* (1861) dazzled Victorian audiences with their remarkable sweep, colour and flair. The former provides a breathtaking view of the falls from water-level as the torrent rushes toward the precipice; the latter offers a stunning recreation of icebergs looming upward in the Arctic night. Panoramas such as these were important visual predecessors to *Titanic*.

Art, of course, is a topic woven through the narrative. Jack is an itinerant artist who has been based in Paris. In one early scene, when he and Rose are becoming acquainted, he shows her his sketchbook. Later he draws her in the nude adorned only with earrings and the Heart of the Ocean (a name, as it happens, reminiscent of Church's *The Heart of the Andes*). The first actual talk of art comes in an early scene as Rose settles into her stateroom with oil paintings purchased on the continent.

There's something wonderfully campy about this scene, given that Rose's recently acquired tableaux by the likes of Degas, Monet and Picasso happen to be world-famous paintings, or close approximations of the same, which today are all prominently displayed in public art museums rather than buried at the bottom of the sea. (Later, a Cézanne still life also appears.) The scene, with a nod and a wink, panders to the late twentieth-century audience's middlebrow knowledge of the history of modern art as a series of rejections of the avant-garde by the philistines of the time. Rose's fiancé Cal, the personification of bourgeois thick-headedness, says of Picasso and his paintings, 'He won't amount to a thing. He won't, trust me. At least they were cheap.' The expectation here is that most audience members – whether they've sat through Modern Art 101 or not – will have enough common knowledge to cluck with amusement at Cal's historical shortsightedness: Who in twentieth-century art ever became more famous and high-priced than Picasso? What might be less widely known is that by 1912 Picasso was already well on his way to being rich and famous, and Degas and Monet, though still active and alive, were by then veritable Old Masters whose paintings of the vintage shown here had been scooped up

years before by American millionaires such as New York's Havermayers and Chicago's Palmers and Fields.

In addition to eliciting chuckles from the viewer whom it has flattered for possessing superior insight and knowledge, the scene accomplishes other purposes. For one, it serves as a shorthand way of sharpening the contrast between Rose (loves art, has vision, takes risks) and her mismatched fiancé (disdains art, lacks vision, is crudely conservative). This early scene, like most that follow, paints Rose and Cal with broad strokes indeed.

But there's another function to the art in the stateroom. Regardless of whether or not Cameron intended it, the paintings shown here provide a pocket history of modern art over the course of four decades, from the Impressionist exhibits of the mid-1870s to the birth of Cubist and abstractionist art around 1910. The Degas depiction of ballerinas, colourfully and loosely painted in the Impressionist manner but also carefully drawn, exhibiting a decisive compositional structure and representational fidelity, gives way to Monet's Post-Impressionist tone poem of water lilies, an image saturated with subjective, non-representational colour and amorphous in structure. Picasso's breakthrough modernist work *Desmoiselles d'Avignon* (1907) rejects Impressionism and Post-Impressionism alike with its flat, unmodulated surfaces, violent forms and agitated concatenation of primitivism,

'Something Picasso. He won't amount to a thing'

archaism and modernity. The fourth painting – similar to Picasso's *Portrait of Ambroise Vollard* (1910) – virtually eschews mimetic representation altogether.

Even though the stateroom scene is set up in such a way as to align the viewer with Rose, who appreciates modern art, and against Cal, who does not, the film as a whole, like virtually all commercial feature films, has little room for the anti-mimetic and anti-narrative trajectory of modern art. Taken collectively, the paintings that Rose brings into her stateroom are firmly opposed to the telescopic / microscopic view of the world perfected by Cameron's artistic forebear Frederic Church. Whereas the modernists strove to flatten the picture space until almost all illusion of pictorial depth was eliminated, Victorians such as Church attempted to stretch pictorial depth to the furthest imaginable reaches. This, too, is Cameron's visual project, particularly in his concern to plunge the viewer viscerally into the depth represented by the enormous length of the ship or, later, its vertiginous height when up-ended in the water.

The conjunction between modern art (Degas, etc.), modern technology (*Titanic*) and the modern woman (Rose) is driven home by the film's use of the metaphor 'stretching her legs' on three separate occasions. First, we see a painted example: the Degas ballerinas stretch their legs in the pursuit of their art and, in effect, the artist's. In the following scene Captain Smith employs the metaphor as a figure of speech about the vessel: 'Take it to sea, Mr Murdoch. Let's stretch her legs.' Finally, when Rose, daring to venture out of the oppressive insulation of her social class, accompanies Jack into steerage and shows her new-found friends her ability to perform a balletic toe stand, she literally stretches her legs – and does so figuratively as well.

A Screwball Tragedy

The best-known book about the *Titanic* disaster is Walter Lord's popular account from 1955, *A Night to Remember*. Coincidentally, that title amalgamates the names of two famous movies that Cameron's *Titanic* draws from: *It Happened One Night* (1934) and *An Affair to Remember*

(1957). The former is a fast-paced romantic comedy about a runaway heiress who falls into the arms of an impecunious but street-smart rover. The latter is a tear-inducing melodrama about a shipboard romance doomed by a series of accidental mishaps. *Titanic* may be classifiable as an historical epic and a disaster movie, but it also derives in a major way from two other movie genres: the screwball comedy and the women's film.

The basic premise of the screwball comedy is this: young A (male or female) is imprisoned within a rigid, humourless, uptight social structure until young B (the gender opposite of A) blows into the picture like a fresh wind and ends up effecting A's release. In *It Happened One Night*, Clark Gable makes it possible for Claudette Colbert to decide against a marriage that's all wrong for her. In *Bringing Up Baby* (1938), madcap Katharine Hepburn sweeps into prim, supercilious Cary Grant's life and upends everything, including his plans for a marriage that's all wrong for him. In *His Girl Friday* (1940), daft newspaper editor Cary Grant brings turmoil into the life of newly retired reporter Rosalind Russell and makes her see that returning to work is a better choice than settling down into marriage with a well-meaning dullard who is, clearly, all wrong for her. In *The Philadelphia Story* (1940), Cary Grant, as Katharine Hepburn's ex-husband, causes Hepburn to drop her stuffed-shirt fiancé, who is patently all wrong for her, and go back to Grant. In *Holiday* (1938), Grant, playing the nonconformist fiancé of Hepburn's snobbish sister, rescues Hepburn from the stultification of her upper-class existence and in the process realizes that the sister to whom he is engaged is, of course, not the right one.

Titanic is no screwball comedy, and Winslet and DiCaprio no Hepburn and Grant. Still, it helps us to understand the nature of the film's romance plot and paper-thin characterizations by recognizing its screwball comedy underpinnings. The screwball genre never for an instant left doubt on the audience's part that young A and B would end up together or that a timely come-uppance would deflate the stuffed shirts and snobs who personified social repression and hypocrisy. Viewers of *Titanic* who have complained about the flat characterizations of the film's heavies, Cal Hockley, his lugubrious valet and Rose's prim and snobby mother, might do well to recall that the counterparts of these figures in the romantic comedies of the 1930s were no less thinly drawn. The very nature of the genre called for characters such as these to be flat and dull; the better to throw into relief the liveliness of the hero and heroine and encourage audiences to enjoy the couple's exuberant displays of anti-authoritarian behaviour.

An essential element of the screwball comedy is the teaching of life skills by the hero to the heroine or vice versa. Hepburn teaches Grant to accept the chaos of life in *Bringing Up Baby*; he teaches her to do cartwheels in *Holiday*. Sometimes the teaching goes both ways. In *It Happened One Night*, Gable teaches Colbert tricks of survival on the open road (how to sleep out of doors), but she shows him how to hitch a ride (as if her technique of lifting up her skirt would work for him!). In *Titanic*, Rose instructs Jack in the ways of high-society table manners, but most of the instruction comes from him, memorably so in the scene, comparable to Gable teaching Colbert how to dunk a doughnut, in which he shows her how to spit. This proletarian gaucherie is played for laughs – when Rose rears back for a big spit from the railing of the first-class deck, she does so just as her snobbish mother and her mother's hoity friends pass by, and when Rose introduces Jack, he has an incriminating glob of spit clinging to his chin. Not subtle, perhaps, but it's in keeping with the romantic comedy conventions invoked by this section of the film. When Hepburn breaks into a cartwheel at the end of *Holiday*, we know that she has finally achieved liberation from the Park Avenue social order that oppressed her. Likewise, when Rose, late in *Titanic*, lets loose with a gob in Cal's face, this physical gesture, learned under Jack's tutelage, graphically exemplifies her emergence from dependence to independence.[23]

The formal dinner scene is a populist set piece in which Jack, in his borrowed tuxedo, matches wits with the exclusionary Cal and Mrs Bukater, and wins the approval of the more benevolent plutocrats at the table for his anthem to the free life. 'You learn to take life as it comes at you – to make each day count,' he says; 'To making it count!' they salute, raising their glasses in toast. The scene concludes when Cal announces that the men will now retire to the library for brandy and cigars. In our

post-feminist era, 'brandy and cigars' is encoded as the domain of male chauvinism, and Cal's dismissive remark to Jack that he needn't join the men because they'll be discussing business and politics is a crude but effective ploy to further the filmgoers' alienation from Cal's patriarchal elitism and to heighten their allegiance to the inevitable romance between Jack and Rose.

Jack teaching Rose to spit; Peter (Clark Gable) teaching Ellie (Claudette Colbert) to dunk a doughnut in *It Happened One Night*

As he leaves the table, Jack passes a secret note to Rose: 'Make it count. Meet me at the clock.' She does, and there he says to her, 'So, you want to go to a real party?' Cut to the revelry of third-class passengers drinking and dancing below decks in steerage. A pick-up band plays frenzied Irish music, and a Slav spins about in a Cossack dance. The scene is like something out of Brueghel or, from an American context, George Caleb Bingham, who painted joyous, unfettered boatmen dancing spirited jigs. The contrast here between first class and steerage is driven home by a cut from a point-of-view shot of Rose spinning deliriously with Jack on the dance floor to a glimpse of her stodgy fiancé ensconced amid brandy and cigars in a room somewhere up above, pontificating on the Sherman Anti-Trust Act. The facile dichotomizing achieved by this cutting is of the sort that made a lot of sense to Depression-era audiences, for whom the screwball comedy provided, along with copious laughs, a reassuring view of the innate vitality and spontaneity of 'the people'. (Even the Marx Brothers played up shipboard contrast in *A Night at the Opera* (1935), with Groucho tweaking the stuffed shirts in the fancy dining room while his brothers make merry amid rollicking immigrant passengers in steerage.) When Rose literally stretches her legs in this scene by performing a toe-stand from classical dance, she is also metaphorically bringing to the table an offering of herself, conveying her as-yet inchoate wish to break free of the over-refined bourgeoisie and join instead the ranks of the great unwashed.

But if the romance in *Titanic* is part *It Happened One Night*, it's also part *An Affair to Remember*, or what was termed in the studio days a 'weepie' or 'women's film'. Targeted by studio heads for specifically female, mostly middle-class audiences, and therefore generally regarded by film critics and other cultural custodians as trashy and beneath serious consideration, the women's film was rediscovered by feminist film critics in the 1970s. These critics and theorists appreciated the way the classic women's pictures not only provided significant professional opportunities for female writers, designers and actors, but also focused attention on female subjectivity and women's real-life concerns about love, family and work. Moreover, as Andrea S. Walsh has written, the women's film

'embodies a key feminist assumption: that women can and should make choices about their lives'.[24]

Thus the women's film – like the screwball comedy, but with an altogether different and ultimately tragic tone – often contained narratives about strong-minded women resisting oppressive patriarchal arrangements and searching for personally meaningful and egalitarian relationships. Bette

Revelry below decks; George Caleb Bingham, *The Jolly Flatboatmen* (Manoogian Collection, Taylor/AKG)

Davis, Joan Crawford and Barbara Stanwyck were quintessential women's picture stars, and often, like Kate Winslet in *Titanic*, they radiated physical strength, even power (unlike other women's picture stars of the 1930s and 1940s, such as Irene Dunn, Joan Fontaine and Margaret Sullavan, whose films played up a physical slightness and vulnerability that they were required to transcend through massive doses of suffering). In *Now, Voyager* (1942), for example, Bette Davis starts off as an ugly duckling suffocating under the excessive control of her domineering mother. Approaching a nervous breakdown, she commits herself to a sanitarium, where an understanding male physician helps her to discover her inner strength. Now transformed into a self-reliant and attractive young woman, she signs up for an ocean cruise and enjoys a passionate if doomed love affair with a married man (who, famously, lights two cigarettes simultaneously and hands one to her). Rose Bukater is no ugly duckling, of course, but the domineering mother whose demands drive her to the brink of suicide, the supportive counsel from a non-predatory male (in this case, Jack), and a

Charlotte Vale (Bette Davis) before her transformation in *Now, Voyager*

passionate shipboard romance (again, with Jack) are ways in which *Titanic* borrows elements from classic women's films such as *Now, Voyager* and rolls them into its own particular configuration.

Typically, the sex objects in women's films were not the female protagonists themselves, but rather spectacularly handsome men who threatened to ruin their lives, either by murdering them (*Rebecca*,

Suave Jack; Cary Grant, with Ingrid Bergman, in *Notorious*

Suspicion, Gaslight, Autumn Leaves), scorning them (*Wuthering Heights, Notorious*), neglecting them (*Back Street, Letter From an Unknown Woman*) or simply dying on them, as is the case in *Titanic*. Usually, the male love object was dark in appearance and often dark in temperament as well: Laurence Olivier, Charles Boyer, Montgomery Clift and the exquisitely versatile actor who was no less at home here than in the screwball comedy, Cary Grant. But dark or fair, the male love object was almost always characterized by emotional sensitivity and emotional or physical vulnerability. Jack Dawson, as played by Leonardo DiCaprio, is both sensitive and vulnerable: sensitive, because he *cares* about Rose and her emotional dilemmas; vulnerable, because physically he seems smaller, thinner and lighter (in both weight and hair colour) than the woman he loves.

It's more than Jack's sensitivity, vulnerability and appearance that draw Rose to him. What most elicits her passion is his capacity for teaching her how to confront her bored and vapid life, take control of it and 'make it count'. In this he embodies the inspirational guidance of Robert Henri ('HEN-rye'), a celebrated bohemian artist and art instructor of the pre-war period during which the film is set. Henri counselled his students to plunge into life, to do and see and observe everything possible with as much passion and candour as they could muster in order to make their own lives into works of art. Urging his students to break free of bourgeois aimlessness and conventionality, which he believed could only result in figurative if not literal suicide, Henri insisted that 'It takes wit, and interest and energy to be happy. ... One must be open and alive. ... There are no easy ruts to get into which lead to happiness.'[25] Henry James proffered similar advice: 'Try to be one of the people on whom nothing is lost!'[26] That is, 'Take each day and make it count.'

When Rose's starchy mother presses at the dinner party, 'And where do you live, Mr Dawson?' his impromptu speech derives not only from Henri and James but also from Emerson and Whitman (author, incidentally, of the phrase 'Now, Voyager') as filtered through Jack London and Jack Kerouac.[27] 'Right now my address is the *RMS Titanic*. After that,

I'm on God's good humour. ... I've got everything I need right here with me. I've got the air in my lungs and a few blank sheets of paper. You learn to take life as it comes at you – to make each day count.'

'Meet me at the clock,' he adds in his secret missive to Rose. This is more than simply a cue to the next scene. It's a counterpoint to the previous imperative, 'Make it count,' in that it's a reminder of temporality and, by extension, mortality. The nuance here is that one can only make it count if one feels time at one's back, for without that tension there's no impetus to make it count. Life is finite, the clock is always ticking, and we must make the most of life before it's too late.

Cameron cuts from a close-up of Jack's handwriting to a point-of-view shot of Rose ascending the Grand Staircase to the landing where Jack waits for her beneath the clock. It is a shot of such importance that it is reprised at the end of the film, the very end, but with an ecstatic time-transcendence that Max Ophuls, the master of such glorious tracking shots, was too much the worldly pessimist to allow in his own masterpieces about love, contingency and time, *Letter from an Unknown Woman* (1948), *The Earrings of Madame de ...* and *Lola Montes* (1955). For Ophuls, time is always running out and can never be recaptured except as a bittersweet longing or recognition of failed opportunities. *Titanic*, however, espouses a different eschatology, in which time can be redeemed by memory, and love, in the end, outruns the clock.

Tight Lacing

From here Cameron cuts to the below-decks dancing scene, with its populist overtones out of Frank Capra and, especially, John Ford, for whom public dancing, as in *The Grapes of Wrath* (1940) or *My Darling Clementine* (1946), figured as a sign of cohesive community. The following morning, Cal breakfasts with Rose, à la *Citizen Kane*, in a solarium and flies into a crystal-smashing rage, again out of *Citizen Kane*, when, in defiance of his orders to stay away from the steerage passengers, she rejoins, 'I'm not a foreman in your mills that you can command. I'm your fiancée.'

Cal's proprietary attitude toward workers and women alike is reiterated in the following scene, in which Mrs Bukater literally, as well as

symbolically, tight-laces her daughter into the confines of a corset. The
Degas painting of Second Empire ballet dancers, themselves figures of a
patriarchal class system that reduces attractive and needy young women
into aesthetic ornaments and objects of desire, pertinently occupies the
space over Rose's shoulder. She, like they, has been stretching her legs, but
they too, like she, were pretty pawns in a game of sexual and economic

Cal and Rose at breakfast; *Citizen Kane*

exchange. When Mrs Bukater explains to Rose that she must submit herself to marriage with Cal because they need the money ('Do you want to see me working as a seamstress?' – another paradigmatic, class-bound female for Degas), Rose protests, 'It's so unfair!' The mother replies, 'Of course it's unfair. We're women. Our choices are never easy.'

The critique of proprietary patriarchy advanced by this scene is furthered in the brief scene that follows, when the high and mighty on *Titanic* join together for the Sunday worship service. Their hymn singing is more than a little pompous and hypocritical, especially when Jack, who attempts to join them in order to see Rose, is locked out by stewards who guard the door.

Admittedly, this and the other 'social consciousness' scenes could be considered evidence of a cynical ploy on the part of the film-makers to exploit female and underclass viewers' indignation toward male and class privilege as a way of broadening the film's audience base. That may well have been an underlying motivation, but what is undeniable is that a populist brand of social criticism is consistent throughout the film. The folk heroine Molly Brown explicitly mocks the pretensions of the wealthy class to which her fabled Colorado gold mines provide access ('Why do they always insist on announcing dinner like a damn cavalry charge?'), Cal sneers at underlings and throws money at them while patronizing his fiancée with the nickname 'Sweet Pea', Jack extols the virtues of the

Pretty pawns in a game of sexual and economic exchange

simple, non-capitalist life ('Just call me a tumbleweed blowing in the wind'), and Rose suggests to *Titanic* magnate Bruce Ismay that he ought to read Freud inasmuch as 'His ideas about the male preoccupation with size might be of particular interest to you.' During the sinking itself, the plight of third-class passengers is dramatically rendered when their escape exits are kept locked by ship stewards zealously intent on guarding the interests of their masters in first class.

Debate still divides historians as to whether this blockage was actually the case, but the locking of steerage passengers below decks ('penned in like cattle' and 'held back in the passageway with loaded revolvers pointed at them') has from the first been a feature of

oppositional, anti-capitalist accounts of the disaster.[28] Which is to say that the class criticism expressed in the film, far from being anachronistic or gratuitous, is consistent with populist and radical perceptions of the catastrophe ever since the US Senate investigation revealed that more than 60 per cent of the first-class passengers were saved as opposed to fewer than 40 per cent of those in second and third class.[29]

The scandalous fact that *Titanic* was short of lifeboats is alluded to in the brief scene that concludes the social-criticism sequence I've been describing. Rose walks along decks with Mr Andrews, the ship designer, and points out that there seem to be too few lifeboats for the number of passengers aboard. Andrews ruefully admits this to be so, explaining that the owners of the shipping company thought that too many lifeboats spoiled the

Penned in like cattle

graceful appearance of the liner. In the words of an indignant news periodical
of the time, 'So much space had to be given to the private promenades, golf
links, [and] swimming pools for the plutocrats aboard that there was no space
left for life-boats when the crash came. Could misdirected ingenuity,
perverted taste and mental and moral insanity go further?'[30]

    Jack, disguised in an overcoat and bowler obviously appropriated
from someone else, turns from the rail and walks up behind Rose. He taps
her on the arm and sweeps her off to a tryst in the empty gymnasium. The
late afternoon light cascading through the windows onto Leonardo
DiCaprio's fetishized face and tresses, his character, Jack, implores Rose
to save herself by abandoning the class structure that is suffocating her:

'They've got you trapped, Rose.' He wants to take her away from all this:
'I know how the world works: I've got ten bucks in my pocket, I have
nothing to offer you and I know that, I understand. But I'm too involved
now. You jump, I jump. Remember?'

    'You jump, I jump' is an allusion to the night when Jack confronted
Rose as she was poised to leap from the aft-deck railing. But now, eyes
primed with tears at the recognition that what he says about her is true,
she resists Jack and his offer. She pushes past him. In the quiet but
perspicacious scene that follows, Rose sits at tea with the other first-class
passengers and silently observes the behaviour of an immaculately
dressed, golden-haired, porcelain-doll of a little girl seated at another
table. There's a resonance here with, of all things, the scene in the Italian

'It was thought – by some – that the deck would look too cluttered' neo-realist masterpiece *Bicycle Thieves* (1948) in which the ill-fed urchin Bruno, the moral centre of the film, can't take his eyes off the mannered behaviour of a pampered little rich boy at a Roman trattoria. Here, the dainty, white-gloved little girl functions as a way of showing that the entrapment or cultural indoctrination of women starts at a very early age. The camera dollies in on Rose as she watches with alarm the child's meticulous folding of the cloth napkin on her lap. In purely visual terms, the bitter truth of Jack's remark, 'They've got you trapped, Rose,' is impressed upon her. Admittedly, the dialogue of *Titanic* is often crude and one-dimensional, but here is an instance of dialogue-free eloquence.

The cut from a close-up of the little girl's folded table napkin, with all its implications of restrictive formality, to an overhead shot of the ship cutting boldly and free through the waves, brilliantly juxtaposes the one manner of life with the other and leads directly to Rose's reappearance on deck, where the open sky and boundless sea provide an almost visceral contrast to the hothouse preciousness she has fled. Thus begins the most purely romantic scene in the film, romantic not only in the sense of being a love scene between the two principals, but also romantic in its affirmation of a heightened reality and place of refuge for those who are able to transcend the stupefying mundanity and grasping greediness of daily life in modern society. Jack is in his symbolic place at the bow railing – the American Adam's future-oriented spot, as opposed to the backward-facing aft railing, from which Rose contemplated suicide. He faces the future and the New World; at his back is the Old World and everything it represents in terms of archaic doctrines and hierarchies. The fresh ocean air caresses his face, which is bathed in the light of the setting sun. Rose approaches. The love theme swells.

Jack tells Rose to close her eyes and trust him. Taking her hand, he guides her onto the railing. She leans into the wind, her arms spread wide. When she opens her eyes, she gasps breathlessly. 'I'm flying, Jack!' she squeals. A great deal of past culture is enfolded in this moment. Rose has become the *Titanic*'s figurehead, the carved female figure traditionally mounted on the prow of a sailing vessel to bring it godspeed and good fortune. She's Wendy to Jack's Peter Pan, exalting in the power he has given her to take flight. The Golden Age of Hollywood is invoked as well: Greta Garbo in period costume staring stoically into the distance from a ship's prow in the classic final shot of *Queen Christina* (1933) or Errol Flynn stout-heartedly gripping the ship's riggings in *Captain Blood* (1935). The cutting of the scene intertwines the lovers' hands and faces, the music swirls around them, the camera soars rapturously, and the last, rose-coloured light of the day bespeaks, in time-honoured fashion, both the romantic ardour of the young couple who are blessed by love and the melancholy of their doomed situation.

The scene ends with a slow dissolve to the rusted bow of the sunken liner some 84 years later. It's a chilling, even terrifying, transition. Like a seventeenth-century Dutch painting that includes a skull in the foreground as a way of reminding viewers that mortality is ever-present, even in the midst of joy and material well-being, the dissolve shows in one prolonged instant the inevitable encroachment of age, decay and death upon nothing less than the most vividly coloured moments of life. Old Rose comments poignantly in voice-over, 'That was the last time *Titanic* ever saw daylight.'

Unlacing

Another dissolve, this from the video monitor image of the ruined stateroom at the bottom of the sea to the same room in pristine condition on the night of the collision. Young Rose appears, dressed as before and holding in her hand Cal's betrothal gift, the Heart of the Ocean. Emboldened by her experience on the bow of the ship, and clearly intent upon asserting independence from her fiancé, she says to Jack, 'I want you to draw me like one of your French girls, wearing this [the necklace]. … Wearing only this.' By 'like one of your French girls', she refers to the sketches of nude models that Jack had shown her on deck the previous day. His reaction to her offer to disrobe indicates his surprise, not that a woman would voluntarily remove her clothes for him, but that *this* woman would, for she is not a woman of his own social class, nor a hired artist's model, but a social superior. As his Irish acquaintance Tommy Ryan remarks the first time Jack sees Rose (standing, significantly, on the deck

Ardent love and the inevitable encroachment of age, decay and death

Captain Blood; Queen Christina

above them), 'Forget it, boyo. You're as likely to have angels fly out of your arse as to get next to the likes of her.'

In terms of the film's sexual politics, Rose is the initiator. She controls her most prized commodity, her body. Cal has insinuated that he wants privileged access to this body before their wedding night, as when he gives her the Heart of the Ocean in her boudoir and pleads 'Oh, open your heart to me, Rose' in a way that clearly conveys it's more than her heart that he's talking about. Her impulse to fling herself off the stern of the ship was prompted by Cal's insistence on his rights to her body, whereas, in a perfectly weighted contrast, her sensation of flying aloft from the bow was prompted by Jack's persistent encouragement to her to attain self-possession.

The erotic charge of the scene that follows results from the fact that the woman, instead of being a passive object of desire, initiates, activates and controls the intimate encounter. Even though she is the one who is reclined naked on a chaise like a voluptuous nude out of Titian, Velázquez or Rubens, the scene is clearly anchored to her eyes, her act of looking, her exercise of will. We see Jack's eyes – intense, serious, professionally engaged – as viewed from her vantage point (the same close-up that flashed before us when old Rose initially encountered the drawing that we only now see being made). Earlier Rose's mother strapped her tightly into a corset, apparel that from before the turn of the century had been

Rose, the initiator

regarded by feminists as a symbol for the restriction of female energy, strength and sexuality. But now the two corsets binding Rose, one literal, the other metaphoric, have been cast aside, and her body is comfortable, relaxed and free. Here it should be noted that the body of the actress playing Rose, Kate Winslet, is actually fleshy in terms of the media-determined standards for female beauty set by 1990s fashion models and film stars, but is just about 'right' by the counterpart mass-media standards of the 1910s. By showing Rose's 'excess' flesh unbounded by stays, the film allows viewers to understand in a visceral way the liberation that has just occurred.[31]

Posing 'like one of your French girls' for Jack, wearing nothing but the Heart of the Ocean, thus allows Rose simultaneously to defy her mother, spurn her fiancé and engage with Jack in a form of safe sex in which she always retains control, being at any moment able to call a halt to the proceedings. She mocks Jack playfully ('So serious!' and 'I can't imagine Monsieur Monet blushing') and lavishes visual attention on his eyes while he, truly so serious, concentrates on the artistic task at hand. In other words, between the two of them, the gaze that appropriates is hers, not his. He, more than she, is the object of the gaze. In truth, however, they *both* are offered up as objects of visual desire for the viewer, who, according to individual preference, may find one a more sexually arousing sight than the other. Of course not every viewer of *Titanic* is bound to have been sexually piqued by Kate Winslet's nakedness or Leonardo DiCaprio's eyes, but that the movie wants and expects this to be the case is suggested by the brief digression from the 1912 narrative to the frame story in a manner that elicits the best laugh of the film.

This is how it happens. The camera moves in on an extreme close-up of Rose's eyes as she gazes at Jack's eyes, and that shot metamorphoses into a matched pull-back of the elderly Rose's eyes as she mentally recalls the scene. The voice-over comes on: 'It was the most erotic moment of my life.' Cutaway to a medium shot of the flabbergasted faces of the 1990s salvage crew. The cut causes audiences to laugh, for it is equivalent to a comic punchline or the payoff panel in a cartoon strip: it abruptly and humorously shifts tone and point of view, allowing for a different perspective, a new spin, on the information that has immediately preceded it. The cut also serves to accomplish what Mark Twain regarded as a necessity for good story-telling: a strategically timed pause that interrupts the narrative at a crucial moment and baits the listener, who can't wait to get on with the story. According to Twain, the pause 'is a dainty thing, and delicate, and also uncertain and treacherous; for it must be exactly the right length – no more and no less – or it fails of its purpose and makes trouble'.[32]

But even more than a Mark Twain-like breach of the story, the cutaway from Jack and Rose to the transfixed salvage crew is a Brechtian moment of alienation. That is, it interrupts the seamless flow of the

dramatic narrative in order to remind the film audience of its own complicity in the illusion being spun. Rose's auditors, lined up in a row and faced forward precisely like filmgoers at *Titanic*, show by their enthralled and even dumbfounded demeanours that each of them has been screening her story in his or her own imagination. A cartoonish look overtakes the listeners as they lean forward, their eyes glazed over and their tongues almost literally hanging out, and rightly so, because the cutaway amounts to a satiric jab at the film audience itself. If this were happening in a European art film directed by Jean-Luc Godard in the 1960s instead of a Hollywood blockbuster directed by James Cameron in the 1990s, such a moment might even be critically esteemed as a playful instance of modernist self-reflexivity.

'It was the most erotic moment of my life'

Perhaps now is the time to note the anachronistic quality of Jack's drawing. From the style of the hair to the disposition of the body to the crudity of outline and shading, the drawing looks more like an old *Playboy* illustration or a nude-on-black-velvet oil painting than a plausible example of sketchwork done in the early part of the century. Granted, Kate Winslet's physiognomy and hair style are not those of a belle *circa* 1912, so a lookalike drawing of her would not, in any case, make for a convincing simulacrum of a sketch from that era. But at least one might have expected a congruity in representational style. The style here is that of late twentieth-century commercial illustration, with the quick legibility and overstated touch that is well-suited to mass reproduction on billboards, magazine ads and, as happens here, multiplex screens, but is far from the style that even commercial illustrators, let alone progressive artists, practised in the early part of the century.

When Jack, in the on-deck scene of the previous afternoon, shows Rose his sketchbook, the images she flips through are for the most part knock-offs of famous twentieth-century photographs, including Alfred Stieglitz's *Georgia O'Keeffe: A Portrait – Hand and Breasts* (1919) and Brassaï's *'Bijou' of Montmartre* (*c*. 1935).[33] It's a strange, ahistorical mixture of sources, and one needn't be a specialist in the history of twentieth-century art and photography to feel that something here is out of whack. For all the ridiculously expensive efforts of Cameron and his design staff to achieve historical authenticity with the reconstruction of the *Titanic* and the costumes of its passengers and crew, historical accuracy with regard to the art has been cast to the wind. Whereas the earlier anachronism of Rose carting aboard a trunkload of Monets, Cézannes and Picassos can be explained simply as a gag or, more intriguingly, as a thematic nod to the history of modernism, what can we possibly make of the gross ahistoricity of Jack's drawings?

Only this. Inadvertently or not, anachronism calls attention to the ahistorical nature of historical pictures in general, regardless of how rigorously they strive for accuracy. Movies set in the past are always, in the final analysis, *about* the present. No matter how serious or devout the film-maker's interest in the historical past, film is a medium of and about that which is contemporary. This is so because movies are made *in* the present *for* the present – the past does not buy tickets. In movies, the historical past is at best a guise, a device, for addressing the present, for catching and holding its interest. Historical accoutrements – not only sets, props and costumes but also dialogue, themes and characterizations – serve as an allegory of the present. Costume pictures proclaim to audiences how surprisingly like us these people were; they may have dressed differently from us, but otherwise they were the same under the skin, and thus their problems, woes and concerns are ultimately identical to our own.

Walter Benjamin, the Marxist philosopher of mass culture, insisted that historicist attempts to reclaim (or, in a term appropriate to *Titanic*, to *salvage*) the past are invariably governed by the dictates of the present. 'Thus, to Robespierre,' he wrote, 'ancient Rome was a past infused with the time of the now which he blasted out of the continuum of history. The French Revolution viewed itself as Rome reincarnate.'[34] Benjamin disdained historicism – 'the romantic gaze into history' and 'the worship

The Terminator

of ruins' – because it pretended to an objectivity, a disinterestedness, it could never achieve. *Titanic* makes no such pretense, despite all the costly costuming and period-accurate sets and the instruction to actors in the etiquette protocols of the time, because every so often it rips aside the scrim of historical veracity with its blatant anachronisms (Rose's art collection, Jack's sketches) and intrusive 1990s colloquialism (the 'no way!' teen talk and facial mugging of the two leads).

Far from attempting to suppress anachronism like a good historicist would, Cameron seems fascinated by it. Indeed, anachronism – the placement of a thing or person outside its proper location in history – is the subject and guiding metaphor of his first hit film, *The Terminator* (1984). The premise of *Terminator* is that the future will make it possible for people (as well as killer robots in pursuit of them) to return to an earlier era, such as our own, in order to undo the historical processes that would otherwise lead to that future. If *Titanic*, unlike *Terminator*, is not about anachronism *per se*, it nevertheless blithely countenances anachronisms and regards them benignly. (Cronos, the Greek embodiment of time, was not a god but a *Titan* – the root word of *Titanic*.)

The most conspicuous of the film's anachronisms occurs immediately after the scene in which Jack draws Rose in the nude. The young couple leaves the stateroom only to discover that Cal's spy, Lovejoy, has spotted them. They race down a corridor and jump into a lift. Its gated doors snap shut and Rose, giggling, *gives her pursuer the finger*. As it happens, though, this is not as much of an anachronism as would appear to be the case. Folk etymologists have traced 'the one-finger salute' as far back in history as the Battle of Agincourt in 1415. But whatever its historical origins, the gesture was deemed a strictly masculine one, a way for military combatants to taunt one another and show disdain. That Rose would be the one to offer the gesture is generally anachronistic, since well-bred women didn't do that sort of thing, but then again historically plausible, given that she is defined as a young woman who is in the process of loosening her stays and transgressing male-dominant authority.

To conservative commentators of the era, the sinking of *Titanic* signalled the precipitous decline of Western civilization and the traditional moral values that had kept it afloat. As Henry Adams observed, 'Our society has politically run on an iceberg, and the confusion and darkness are fatal.'[35] Rose's rebellious and unladylike actions – running, giggling, flipping the finger, not to mention exhibiting herself nude to a man who is neither her husband nor a member of her social class – constituted exactly

Jacques-Louis David, *Madame Récamier* (1800, Musée du Louvre/AKG): the romantic gaze into history; an anachronistic finger?

the sort of behaviour that conservatives liked to point to when charging modern women with civilization's decline or reassuring one another of men's moral superiority.[36] Although *Titanic*, allying itself with progressive politics, presents Rose as a sympathetic and appealing figure, it is structured in such a way as to link her running wild to events themselves running amok as the ship, steaming ahead far too fast and without proper lookout, rushes heedlessly toward its iceberg.

Hot and Cold

The elevator reaches the lowest level of the ship. Pursued by Jack, Rose races through the boiler rooms in a flowing gown. Here is the industrial underworld glimpsed earlier. Grimy labourers heave coal into flame-belching iron furnaces. Seen from behind, her cool gray and white dress, ghostly and ethereal, is strikingly out of place, as though an angel were fleeing through hell. The visual power of this image is offset by Jack's puerile aside to the stokers, 'Don't mind us, you're doing a great job.'

Through the boiler rooms and into the hold, they come upon a sparkling new automobile, the custom-made Renault that was being hauled aboard the ship in the bustling Southampton scene during which young Rose in her purple hat was introduced as a glamorous and costly commodity herself. Now it is tethered in place like a museum object on display. Still the sheltered upper-class girl, Rose climbs into the roofed-over passenger compartment of the car while Jack, the tumbleweed who sleeps beneath the stars, hops into the unroofed driver's seat. Working the wheel and affecting the manners of a chauffeur, he inquires 'Where to, Miss?' She leans forward and whispers in his ear, 'To the stars.' With that, she physically drags him by his arms back into her space. The scene is intended to be romantic and sexually playful, of course, but it is also consistent with the theme of crossing or transgressing class divides that has threaded its way through the film.

It also demonstrates, as before, Rose's growing ability to take control. She, not Jack, initiates the sex that is about to occur. This time he's only the adverb; she's the verb. She kisses his fingers. She tells him,

'Put your hands on me, Jack.' She doesn't so much give herself to him, to use the stock phrase, as take him.

In an allusion to the sexual euphemisms of old films, Cameron cuts to an exterior long shot of the mighty liner on the dark ocean and then again to a close shot of the ship's bow – Jack's space – phallically penetrating the water. Cut to two sailors aloft in the crow's nest on watch. These cuts take us from the lowest occupied space on the *Titanic* to the highest. They take us from warmth and steam (both literal and figurative) into the frigid night air, and from a heterosexual couple in embrace to a homosocial couple embraced only by the tight confines of their lookout post.

Cut again to the steamed-up window of the car. These instances invoke what used to be described as 'the Lubitsch Touch', in honour of

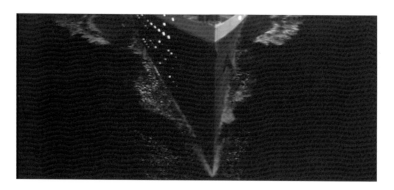

'Where to, Miss?' – 'To the stars'; penetration

Ernest Lubitsch, the director of sparkling sex comedies of the 1930s such as *Trouble in Paradise* (1932) and *Design for Living* (1933). Lubitsch was skilled at deploying censorship-evading visual devices that conveyed through innuendo the sexual intercourse of his characters: at the moment of their embrace he would cut away to silhouettes cast suggestively over a chaise lounge, or he would leave the room altogether and impishly film the closed door. Here, with the camera positioned outside the car, Rose's hand suddenly slams up against the rear window. As it slowly descends again, it wipes a trail against the steamy glass. Inside, the two friends, now lovers, are hot and flushed. Jack, the thinner and more epicene of the two, lies cradled in her arms, reinforcing the impression that Rose has become the dominant figure in their relationship, or at least his equal. Significantly, it is she, not he, who remarks, 'You're trembling.' He lays his head upon her chest.

The mating sequence ends with Cal discovering Jack's drawing of Rose, along with her note, 'Darling, now you can keep us both locked in your safe.' Lovejoy looks on, awaiting his master's bidding. At this point, the narrative of the film turns fugal, with three intertwined strands: Rose and Jack, Cal and Lovejoy, crew and passengers. At any given moment of screen time, one strand is dominant, but in terms of Cameron's story-telling, each has bearing on the others.

Rose is giddy when she and Jack appear on deck in the cold night air. Suddenly she is serious: 'When this ship docks, I'm getting off with you.' This is crazy, he replies. 'I know. It doesn't make any sense. That's

The Lubitsch touch

The convergence of the twain; Arnold Böcklin, *Island of the Dead* (Berlin, SMPK, Nationalgalerie/AKG)

why I trust it.' Hungrily, they kiss. As banal as this interchange may be, it condenses into a few phrases the teen-romance ideology of the film. Whatever else it may be, *Titanic* is a 'teen pic' chronicling the travails of young lovers as they struggle to find their way in a cold, convention-ridden society. Like the fugitive or outcast teen lovers in *Rebel Without a Cause* (1955), *Splendor in the Grass* (1961) and *West Side Story* (1961), Jack and Rose dream of a utopian 'Somewhere', a place where they can elude adult hypocrisy and the unbearable clan pressure that impinges upon them. Little do they suspect that impingement of an altogether different order is about to occur.

In one of the most visually arresting moments in a film replete with such moments, the two sailors aloft, distracted by the kiss on the deck, suddenly look up to see an implacable iceberg looming ahead. The sky is darkest blue, the iceberg black. There's an eerie silence and a massive ominousness similar to that of Arnold Böcklin's famous nocturnal image *Island of the Dead* (1883), in which a boat bearing a mysterious figure clad in

Rebel Without a Cause

white glides across night-stilled waters into the maw of towering granite cliffs. In both cases the moment is charged with awesome inevitability – the inevitability of death in the painting and of deadly collision in the film. Over the next minute or two of screentime, a couple more visually stunning cutaways to the bow on its course with destiny hammers home the point.

Inevitability is the theme of Thomas Hardy's 1912 poem about the crash, 'The Convergence of the Twain'. Hardy imagines two separate but concurrent realms of activity. In the one, humanity fashions the great ocean-going vessel; in the other, nature slowly accretes the even greater mountain of ice: 'And as the smart ship grew / In stature, grace, and hue, / In shadowy silence grew the Iceberg too.' While innumerable commentators at the time blamed the collision on improper management of affairs ('the twin gods of Mammon, *speed* and *greed*'), Hardy thought the accident instead to be cosmically foreordained. Of the ship and the iceberg he writes 'they were bent / By paths coincident / On being anon twin halves of one august event, / Till the Spinner of the Years / Said "Now!" And each one hears, / And consummation comes, and jars two hemispheres.'[37]

Hardy's poem is pointedly sexual. In the opening stanzas the ship is characterized as a vain and glamorous female absorbed in worldly pleasure. The iceberg is her 'sinister mate'. The two experience an 'intimate welding' (or 'wedding'), the 'consummation' of which is nothing short of earth-shaking ('jars two hemispheres'). Cameron's movie also associates the hemisphere-jarring embrace of ship and ice with the sexual embrace of woman and man. Rose's decision to jettison her conventional, pre-arranged life for one of bohemian open-endedness is thus, by association, epochal and hemisphere-jarring.

In an interview, Cameron states, 'There's a moment on the deck of the ship where Rose kisses Jack and tells him when the ship docks she's going with him. She's made a decision that will, in a sense, destroy her world and lead her into his. And it's at that exact moment that the ship rams the iceberg.' He adds, 'The lookouts in the crow's-nest are diverted by Jack and Rose kissing. The distraction is but a few seconds, but critical.... . Rose's moment of greatest free will is the moment that seals her fate, as well as everyone else's on the ship.'[38]

Thus, in Cameron's film, the convergence of the twain is not only that of ship and iceberg, but also of the fictive story line and the historical one. And further, insofar as Rose symbolizes modernist sensibilities shrugging off sexual repression and neo-feudal marital obligation, the collision that her behaviour helps cause is not only with the iceberg but with the solidly frozen social and behavioural codes that the early twentieth-century modernists struggled so hard to shatter. In this regard, the cataclysmic impact shown here is but a vivid metaphor for what art critic Robert Hughes, in a book on modernism, has called 'the shock of the new'.[39]

Frenzy of the Visible

Now, for the first time, *Titanic* becomes exactly what it was expected to be, an action movie. The term *action movie* is ambiguous as a film category, because in theory it encompasses a variety of different genres, among them the western, the crime thriller, the war film and the horror picture. In general, action movies are those that make a spectacle of thrilling, often violent, and typically male-oriented actions such as car chases, punch-ups, shoot-outs, rocket launchings, swordfights, airborne dogfights and so forth. The key to a good action movie is getting the viewer's adrenaline to pump and keep on pumping, and in the 1980s and 90s no film-maker was more successful at this than James Cameron. 'Fear is a very strong reaction,' Cameron has observed. 'It makes people realize that they're alive. Their hearts start to beat faster.'[40]

In *Titanic*, as in *Aliens*, Cameron takes his sweet time setting up the action. *Aliens* was the 1986 sequel to Ridley Scott's 1979 horror-in-outer-space suspense hit, *Alien*, and Cameron knew that fans of the earlier film would come to his movie expecting to be rocked out of their seats from the moment they took them. Therefore, in one of the great tease acts of the modern cinema, he postponed any serious action for a full hour, ensuring that his viewers were practically panting for it by the time it arrived – and arrive it did, in a non-stop way, until the last hairy twist in the roller coaster was finally reached. The same narrative device of prolonged build-up is used in *Titanic*. True, there is one thrilling incident early on, when Rose, having changed her mind about suicide, accidentally falters at the aft-deck railing and has to be prevented from tumbling into the abyss by Jack in a cliffhanger moment straight out of the Mount Rushmore finale of *North By Northwest* (1959). But otherwise all is delay of gratification and frustration of expectation until finally the iceberg is sighted some 100 minutes into the film.

Rose holding on to Jack; *North by Northwest*

When the watchmen spot the monstrous obstacle ahead, they desperately clang the alarm and call down to the bridge. The cutting from shot to shot is fast here, even urgent, as is the music. A helmsman desperately pulls at the wheel, and a cup of tea (symbol for audiences of British calm, orderliness, unflappability) ominously lurches on its saucer. The great liner heads directly for the iceberg, while the rapid editing and the use of handheld camera – associated in the modern viewer's mind with rough and jerky, on-the-spot documentary news reporting – convey a sensation of frantic struggle on the part of the crew to avert disaster. In the industrial underbelly of the ship, the proletarians contend against the *Modern Times* engines with Herculean effort, and an underwater shot reveals the ship propellers reversing direction. The music now becomes low, insistent, powerful.

The ranking officer on deck, Murdoch, urges his leviathan in a tense whisper, 'Come on, come on. Turn.' And, indeed, the ship veers from course and seems to pass safely to the side of the monolithic obstruction by the slenderest of margins. But icebergs, just like good movies, expand outward beneath the surface. The hull of the *Titanic* scrapes against this underwater extrusion and tears a gash 300 feet long. The prolonged kiss between Jack and Rose is broken into by the violence of the collision.

Were this a comedy, the pairing of kiss and crash would amount to a gag. Were it a cautionary tale about the consequences of under-aged sex, the conjunction of the two would be used as a moralistic warning against illicit or improper sexual activity. (Teenagers couple in the back seat of a car and look what happens!) But, instead, this is an historical romance, and so the precise simultaneity of the kiss and the crash adheres to the governing rule of historical fiction, which is that public and historically significant events are best understood by taking measure of the private and personal struggles of fictitious characters put forth as ordinary people whose lives happen to be directly affected by those events.

In his influential study *The Historical Novel* (1937), Georg Lukács, a member of the Hungarian Communist Party, championed the work of bourgeois and politically conservative historical novelists such as Balzac and Scott. He admired these and other historical romancers because, by focusing upon the precise social milieu of their characters, they drew the reader's attention to the complex interaction of social classes that drove the particular society in question. The novelists' political and class affiliations were, in the end, less significant for Lukács than their accomplishment at depicting and examining real-world social structures through the interaction of fictional personages. When Tolstoy's characters witness the burning of Moscow by the retreating French or Stendhal's hero staggers in a daze at the margins of the Battle of Waterloo, the historical novelist is doing more than simply transforming a world-famous event into a dramatic spectacle to be avidly consumed by readers. He or she is reproducing the event *as experienced* through the class-specific and history-bound perceptions of various characters, thus enabling readers to see that event in terms of the larger historical and social processes of which the characters themselves are a part. By linking the fateful encounter with the iceberg to Rose's rejection of her own social class, the film interweaves personal and public cataclysms, situating them both in an historical matrix.

Or, to look at this phenomenon from a different angle, Jack, with all his advice to Rose to live life to the fullest and make it count, is the embodiment of the modern therapeutic culture of consumption that, during the era in which the film is set, took over from the older culture of repression, delayed gratification and patriarchal domination. In the early decades of the century there was a powerful confluence of bohemian imperatives to young people to discover and satisfy their inner natures through art, sex, drinking and dancing, and commercial imperatives for them to do the same through consumption.[41] This 'ensnaring' of modern youth by the twin evils of bohemianism and commercialism was an historical occurrence that, in the eyes of traditionalists and conservatives, was a catastrophe equivalent to the sinking of the great unsinkable ship and the duly hierarchical society it was widely seen as representing.

After Rose and Jack's embrace is jarred by the collision, diamond-like shards of ice spill onto the deck, and water begins to rush into the gash in the ship's hull. A cut then reveals the fancy automobile – the site of their social role-playing and her sexual initiative – being washed away. Another cut shows the stokers scurrying through the fast-flooding boiler

Disaster as spectacle; class analysis

rooms in search of safety. Most of them are able to get away before the watertight steel doors seal off these bulkhead compartments from the rest of the ship, but not everyone makes it. On the musical soundtrack, a lone trumpet repeats a single dark-timbre note anxiously, tentatively, suspensefully.

A breathtaking exterior long shot shows the great liner foundering in the darkness, its clustered lights reflecting off the black waters with an ironic twinkle of merriment. The aesthetic pleasure of this extraordinary sight – a sumptuous, iconic rendition of historical disaster as awesome spectacle – is displaced by an interior shot of hoards of rats scurrying up the third-class corridors in search of safety from the advancing water. With a slight upward tilt, the camera reveals a phalanx of steerage passengers following the rats' lead. Says Tommy Ryan in a statement meant to drive home the film's class analysis, 'If this is the direction the rats are going, that's good enough for me.' The analogy thus made between the rats and the poor is complicated by a cut to ship owner Bruce Ismay, who has rat-like features and even a whiskery moustache. Some are treated like rats, the cutting implies, while others simply are rats.

A Night to Forget

'But this ship can't sink!' the disbelieving Ismay says to ship designer Andrews, who replies, 'She's made of iron, sir. I assure you she can, and she will. It is a mathematical certainty.'

From here *Titanic* increasingly coincides with the 1958 British film about the disaster, Roy Baker's *A Night to Remember*. Indeed, there are so many similarities that partisans of the earlier movie have thought James Cameron excessive in his borrowings. Two important points about this need be made. First, all the incidents that figure into both films – for example, the band playing on or Benjamin Guggenheim preferring his dinner jacket to a life jacket – are well-known occurrences and, as such, belong not exclusively to the earlier film but to the historical event itself, or at least to the lore about it. Second, there is a world of ideological difference between the British film and its Hollywood successor. *A Night to Remember* is very much a product of post-war, post-colonial England.

Probably the chief focus of interest in the film is not the many private tragedies and sorrowful partings that occur but rather the unfortunate communications foul-ups and lack of preparedness that led to such an unnecessary loss of life. Indeed, adapted from Walter Lord's 1955 best-seller by the spy novelist Eric Ambler, *A Night to Remember* seems concerned above all with issues of coded communication, miscommunication, bungled communication and garbled communication. Numerous scenes take place in the offices of the wireless operators on the *Titanic* and two other ships, the nearby *Californian* and the 50-mile-away *Carpathia*. When the operator on the *Californian* repeatedly attempts to notify his counterpart on *Titanic* of ice pack in the area, he can't get through because the *Titanic* wireless is tied up with personal and financial communications fired off by rich passengers. Later, when a warning message does come through, it's inadvertently buried beneath a stack of frivolous messages and thus fails to accomplish its purpose. Later still, when the *Titanic* has begun to list, the wireless operator on the *Californian* has called it a night and gone to sleep. One of his shipmates takes a listen, but as he does not properly understand Morse code, he shrugs his shoulders and switches off the unit. When the *Titanic* sends up distress flares, the watch on the *Californian* assumes that some sort of party must be going on. After enough rockets have been fired to concern him, he calls down to his captain, who grumbles at being awakened. He orders his men to flash a beam of light at the *Titanic* in code inquiring if all is well, but the watch on the *Titanic* is unable to decode the signal. And so it goes until the ship sinks.

Obviously, the obsession with miscommunication and failed warning systems was a meaningful concern to a nation of filmgoers who only a dozen or so years before had relied heavily upon early-warning systems in order to survive the nightly blitz and threat of Nazi rockets. In 1956 the British government installed a new early-warning system against nuclear attack: members of the Royal Observer Corps were to be spread around the country at 15 mile intervals, linked by an underground telephone line that would enable them to spread the word about incoming missiles. Here was a context in which *A Night to Remember*'s concern with

safety and communication was timely and meaningful. In *Titanic*, by contrast, it's barely a side issue. This is not surprising given that today we live in an age of instantaneous global telecommunication, where the least of our worries has to do with urgent information travelling too slowly.

In sum, *A Night to Remember* blames the terrible tragedy not on greed, stupidity or hard-heartedness, but on the misrouting or misunderstanding of essential information. When Captain Smith learns of the appalling shortage of lifeboats on board, he stoically replies, 'I don't think the Board of Trade regulations visualized this situation.' As a matter of historical fact, the *Titanic* did indeed carry the minimum number of lifeboats required by outdated safety codes. Thus, as the 1950s film would have it, the shortsightedness that led to such an unnecessary loss of life was bureaucratic and administrative, not moral and corporate. By contrast, in *Titanic*, when Rose asks Andrews about the shortage of lifeboats, he sighs that the White Star Line wanted them kept to a minimum for purposes of speed and aesthetics (and, by implication, profit).

For all its cautionary concern with communicative and administrative shortcoming, *A Night to Remember* is partisan towards the ship's officers of the *Titanic*. Indeed, the film is far more their story than that of the passengers, who for the most part remain unnamed representatives of social classes and types: the grumpy old dowager, the kindly Jewish couple, the romantic young lovers, the nuclear-family parents and so forth. (The real-life passengers upon whom these figures are based had names, of course, but here they are withheld.) The nearest the film has to a protagonist is Second Officer Lightoller, played by the stolid Kenneth More, best known at the time for his role as the disabled RAF fighter pilot Douglas Bader in the 1956 biopic *Reach for the Sky*. More's Lightoller is humane, dedicated, professional, and is even permitted at the end to voice a modernist or existentialist doubt: 'I don't think I'll ever feel sure again about anything,' he muses from his lifeboat in the dark.

But like Captain Smith and most of the other officers and gentlemen depicted in the film, Lightoller abundantly displays the stiff upper lip in the face of disaster that was an abiding source of national pride (or fantasy) for the English at a time when both at home and abroad Britannia was faced with a series of setbacks. Dunkirk, Singapore and other crushing defeats during the war, and Cyprus, Suez and the disintegration of empire after the war had given the British much practice at stiffening the upper lip. It's the virtue par excellence in *A Night to Remember*, whereas there's little of it to be seen in *Titanic*, inasmuch as stiff-upper-lipping is not widely regarded as a virtue in the therapeutic culture that modern America has become.

In contrast to its reverent treatment of officers, *A Night to Remember* does not hesitate to mock or otherwise denigrate some of the lower-class seamen and stewards aboard the liner. After the collision the baker gets himself drunk and bumbles along comically, and a sailor ineptly wrestles with two collapsible deck chairs that he attempts to tie together into his own private life raft. One scurrilous seaman tries to make off with the chief

A Night to Remember

purser's life preserver and is knocked unconscious for it, another beats away hapless swimmers who climb aboard his overturned lifeboat, while a third, a cockney quartermaster in charge of a lifeboat full of women, refuses Molly Brown's insistence that they row back to pick up survivors. This particular incident is repeated in *Titanic* and is the only occasion in that film in which a working-class figure is singled out for rebuke.

At the end of *A Night to Remember*, the captain of the *Carpathia*, the vessel that was too far away to be of assistance, remarks about the search for survivors, 'Everything that was humanly possible has been done.' These words are ironic, of course, because the film has argued that many things humanly possible could have been done to *avoid* the tragedy in the first place. As the camera looks down at an ocean littered with the detritus of the disaster – deck chairs, a bass fiddle, a child's rocking horse – and 'Nearer, My God, to Thee' sounds mournfully in orchestral rendition, an epilogue scrolls across the screen. Its phrases can be understood as having a secondary meaning in terms of the Cold War politics of the era in which the film was released: '*But this is not the end of the story – for their sacrifice was not in vain* [echoes of Churchill's stirring speech about the heroes of the Battle of Britain and, more generally, the wartime dedication of the British people].' The music suddenly resolves into a triumphal major key at the following lines: '*Today there are lifeboats for all* [i.e. post-war England is a free and egalitarian society]. *Unceasing radio* [and, by extension, radar] *vigil and, in the North Atlantic* [or, more specifically, the countries belonging to the North Atlantic Treaty Organization], *the international ice patrol* [or NATO's 'Cold' War forces] *guards the sea lanes making them safe for* [democracy and] *the peoples of the world.*'

If *A Night to Remember* can be seen as a Cold War fable about the need for preparedness and competent military and class leadership, what sort of post-Cold War fable is *Titanic*? James Cameron has said that fear of nuclear holocaust has haunted him ever since he was a child and that this fear often manifests itself in his films.[42] Although it is a period piece, *Titanic*, too, envisions holocaust. It portrays a pre- and post-apocalyptic world in microcosm. Here it is not aggressor nations or alien races that are to blame for the devastation wreaked upon *Titanic*'s passengers, but rather stupidly greedy capitalists and profiteering corporations. Much in tune with the sentimental liberalism and populism of the Clintonian US in the late 1990s, *Titanic* preaches a doctrine of corporate responsibility toward consumers. Moreover, in the figures of Bruce Ismay and Cal Hochley, it vilifies the very masters-of-the-universe deregulators and entrepreneurial types who only a short time before, in the heady era of Reagan and Bush, had been trumpeted as American heroes.

To the Lifeboats

The next section of the film interpolates the Rose and Jack melodrama into the evacuation story. Cal alerts the Master of Arms that the diamond necklace has been stolen from his safe. When the lovers appear, having come back to the first-class stateroom to warn Rose's mother that the ship is going to sink, Lovejoy slips the allegedly missing pendant into the young man's jacket pocket moments before he is to be searched. Jack's protests of innocence notwithstanding, Rose is temporarily misled into believing that he has betrayed her trust. This is obviously a dramatic hiccup intended to complicate the boy-meets-girl story and send it into its boy-loses-girl phase.

Jack is led away in custody, taken to the bowels of the ship where he will be locked to a metal pipe and guarded over by Lovejoy with his nickel-plated revolver. Above decks, meanwhile, the evacuation of the ship commences. Rose's mother, the full-fledged snob, asks, 'Will the lifeboats be seated according to class?' Voicing the sentiments of the audience, Rose snaps, 'Oh, Mother, shut up!' Then she adds, 'Don't you understand? … Half of the people on this ship are going to die.' This gives Cal the opportunity to prove himself a full-fledged pig: 'Not the better half,' he responds. A distress flare bursting into the sky overhead reveals his betrothed's features in a harsh and blanching light, signaling her full recognition now of his baseness. 'You unimaginable bastard,' she sneers.

Rose refuses to join her mother in a lifeboat, insisting instead that she must find Jack. Cal rails at her for this, accusing her of becoming the other man's whore. 'I'd rather be his whore than your wife,' she replies, whereupon he shakes her violently. With that, she hawks noisily and spits prodigiously in his eye, repaying him for his disrespect and at the same time paying off the much earlier scene in which Jack teaches her how to spit. Chekhov once cautioned that a playwright mustn't show the audience a gun in the first act without it going off in the third. Here, instead of a gun, there's a wad of spit. This is a crowd-pleasing scene, and rightly so, for not only does it exemplify Rose's character evolution (or, from the conservative perspective, de-evolution), it also provides a satisfying moment of dramatic symmetry and resolution in the midst of rising tension and uncertainty with regard to the fate of the various passengers.

Rose dashes off in search of Jack. The uniformed steward standing in front of a lift says, 'I'm sorry, Miss. The lifts are closed.' She shoves him inside and, in typically anachronistic-sounding dialogue, explains, 'I'm through being polite, goddammit.' This is Rose's new tone, like it or not. No sweet young thing, she. No sweet pea. This night to remember has transformed her into a woman that some would call spirited or plucky, and others would call pushy and quarrelsome.

At the F-level deck, following directions given to her by Mr Andrews, she works her way through a maze of corridors. She finds Jack chained to the pipe but can't locate a key with which to unlock him. While she's searching, he asks, 'Rose, how did you find out I didn't do it [steal the diamond]?' Cut to a close-up of Rose. 'I didn't,' she answers. 'I just realized I already knew.' The film's underlying ideology about the transcendence of romantic love over material contingency is articulated here, as is its secondary theme about the superiority of fiction to non-fiction as a means of discerning the truth about people. Rose's instinct or intuition or inherent Neoplatonic recognition of true forms has overruled the false evidence of the senses, as manipulated by Cal and Lovejoy, and allowed her to grasp the reality of the situation.

During the Reformation, the Protestant sect known as the Antinomians rejected the legitimacy of civil law when they found it to be in conflict with intuitively understood moral law. Like student protesters of the 1960s and other civil disobedients before and since, Rose is a latter-day Antinomian, privileging her personal intuition of justice over the due process of law. Her recognition of Jack's innocence despite the evidence brought against him self-authorizes her to release him from his bonds. A gesture of this nature makes perfect sense to a modern-day film viewing audience that accepts in theory, if not in practice, the civil disobedience discourse ('let your conscience be your guide') of a pro-choice, pro-consumer, post-Cold War market society.

Rose runs along the deserted lower corridors of the ship shouting for help. This and the subsequent corridor scenes have a Stanley Kubrick quality about them. Antiseptically white and empty, the corridors stretch on and on in a nightmarish manner, as in *2001: A Space Odyssey* (1968) or *The Shining* (1980). The architectural space is oppressive in its banality and inability to offer refuge. It's also confusing. Each corridor so much resembles the one before and after it that the person passing through is quickly disoriented and trapped, as if in a nefarious labyrinth.

The hallway lights momentarily go dim, increasing the fright factor. We hear Rose's heavy, anxious breathing. This is pure Kubrick, who, in his films, repeatedly relied upon the sounds of anxious breathing to convey the stress and loneliness felt by characters and displace these feelings onto the audience. Rose comes upon a steward, who seems completely out of place, and asks that he come down with her to F deck and help her release Jack. Terrified by the rising flood, he refuses and makes his move to leave. This is not only Kubrick, it's Lewis Carroll: Rose as Alice, having tumbled down a hole into a disturbingly topsy-turvy world. The bolting steward's eyes, if not his mouth, all but cry out, 'I'm late, I'm late, for a very important date.' Rose hauls off and punches him in the face (not a very Alice-like response). 'To hell with you,' he says, and scurries away.

She breaks a fire axe out of a glass case and hefts it in her arms, as she heads back down to rescue Jack. When she plunges off a stairway into the water that is now filling the F-deck corridor, she gasps at how cold it is. This is a payoff for Jack's much earlier comment, at the time of her contemplated suicide, that the water temperature was so low that it would feel like a thousand knives stabbing at her flesh. She pushes ahead through the watery corridor while horrible loud mechanical sounds thump all around her. She is in the belly of the tormented beast, and its innards are roaring with pain.

The scene of breaking Jack's shackles is played for a tension-relieving laugh, but it nevertheless abounds in cultural references and resonances. Physically incapacitated by the bonds that bind him to the pipe while the frigid waters swirl higher and higher, *he*, not she, occupies the position of the distressed damsel needing to be rescued from the fiery dragon, or the fair maiden tied to the railroad tracks. But he is not mentally incapacitated. Ever Rose's instructor in the ways of the world, he advises her as how to wield the axe properly and set him free. The laugh comes when Jack, after asking Rose to take a practice swing against a wooden bureau, tells her to swing again and make the axe head land in the same spot. She doesn't even come close, but with the water rising higher, there's no opportunity for further refinements of technique.

The breaking of handcuffs or leg-irons has featured in numerous escaped-prisoner films over the decades. In the case of the Civil Rights message movie, *The Defiant Ones* (1958), where a black escaped convict is shackled to a white one, the very act itself represents a blow against racial injustice. Here, though, as throughout *Titanic*, racial injustice is not at issue. But gender and class injustices are, and Rose's unlocking of Jack's literal shackle amounts to a reciprocal act for his more abstract unlocking of her social and psychological bindings ('It was the ship of dreams to everyone else. To me it was a slave ship – taking me back to America in chains').

She trembles at what she is about to do, and this is hardly surprising, given her inability to come anywhere near the target with her

In the belly of the beast

second swing. *Star Wars* (1977) to the rescue. Playing Jedi Master Obi-Wan Kenobi to Rose's Luke Skywalker, Jack tells her he trusts her and that she must trust herself in order to bring the axe/lightsabre to rest at its proper place. All that's missing is the admonition 'Let the Force be with you'. Thus Rose's Antinomian trust in her intuition about Jack's innocence is paired with the sort of Hollywoodized version of *Zen in the Art of Archery* that George Lucas and his disciples preached in the science-fiction blockbusters of the 1970s and 80s. The Lucas film marked a turning point for Cameron: 'I was really upset when I saw *Star Wars*,' he has said about a time when he was an aspiring film-maker. 'That was the movie I wanted to make. After seeing that movie I got very determined. I decided to get busy.'[43]

Titanic is like *Star Wars* in other ways besides its adherence to the Eastern and Romantic doctrines of trusting feeling over reason. There is the shared fascination with and brilliance at special-effects technology and a similarly reductive and archetypal approach to characterization. Yet another parallel occurs in terms of cinema literacy. *Star Wars* is encyclopaedic in its allusions to the classics of the world cinema, quoting from sources as diverse as *The Searchers* (1956), *The Seven Samurai* (1954) and *The Triumph of the Will* (1936). Although Cameron, unlike Lucas, is not a film-school product, he too displays a remarkable capacity for telling his story through borrowings and quotations from earlier cinematic stories – what almost amounts to a cinematic version of 'sampling', the procedure used by hip-hop musicians to

Rose poises the axe for a second whack at the wooden bureau

lift entire tracks from earlier recordings by other artists.

But if George Lucas was a tremendous influence on the young
Cameron, Kubrick was another and even earlier one. Cameron says that
after seeing *2001* as a 15-year-old, 'I went back to see the movie ten times
trying to get inside it.'[44] Kubrick's dark, dystopian and paranoid vision of
the world is the yang to Lucas's yin, for in Kubrick good never triumphs
over evil, and is often, in fact, simply evil in disguise. Let's go back to Rose
splintering that wooden bureau with her axe. The action is treated
comically, as explained above, and meant to serve a good purpose, that of
liberating Jack from his bonds before it's too late. In Kubrick's *The
Shining*, the psychotic wife-abuser played by Jack Nicholson chops his way
through a bedroom door that is the only obstacle between him and his
terrified spouse. In *Titanic* the axe is a benevolent instrument swung
through the air on behalf of the heterosexual pairing rather than against it.
Moreover, the bearer of the axe is female.

The Shining

In American lore, the wielding of an axe has always been regarded as a definingly male activity. The yeoman farmer clearing his land of trees, the rugged woodsman felling forests, Abe Lincoln splitting rails, giant Paul Bunyan slinging his axe over his shoulder – axing was thought quintessentially masculine. When women grabbed hold of axes, the natural and social order went awry: Carrie Nation, the turn-of-the-century temperance agitator, smashed saloons with her hatchet, and Lizzie Borden, although acquitted of the charges of double-murder brought against her in 1892, remains to this day infamous for having given her father and stepmother '40 whacks' with her axe.

Cameron reversed this negative stereotype in two of his previous hits. Ripley in *Aliens* and Sarah Connor in *Terminator 2* are women warriors portrayed, not as demented for their desire and ability to wield an axe (or its science-fiction, heavy-metal equivalent), but actually heroic. Although different from them in so many ways, Rose nonetheless is their sister of the blade.

Something You Don't See Every Day

Molly Brown looks on at the sinking *Titanic* from the relative calm and safety of a lifeboat. The ship is tilted at a 45-degree angle, rising from the sea like the blade of a penknife out of its case. It sparkles with myriad lights reflecting in the water and there's a sense of great stir and activity aboard, although from the distance all of that is too far off to be felt as the turbulence and chaos that it really is. The scene is nothing short of

Terminator 2

spectacular. Molly remarks, to no one in particular, 'Now there's something you don't see every day.'

Once again, Cameron's film strikes a self-reflexive note, for we viewers of *Titanic*, quietly lined up in rows and looking raptly ahead, just like Molly Brown and the other lifeboat passengers, behold a spectacle far more impressive than anything normally to be seen either in real life or on a cinema screen. The words 'Now there's something you don't see every day' apply equally well to the stricken ocean liner and to the behemoth of a film that has had both the audacity to re-create that fabled disaster and the technical wizardry to do so in such a convincing and compelling manner. But in this regard, the film simply proves itself to be the latest in a long line of stupendous large-scale cinematic re-creations of the historical past that harkens back through the great Samuel Bronson-produced epics of the 1960s (*El Cid* [1961] and *Fall of the Roman Empire* [1964]), the bloated Biblical sagas of the 1950s (*The Ten Commandments* [1956] and *Ben-Hur* [1959]), David O. Selznik's *Gone with the Wind* (1939), MGM's silent *Ben-Hur* (1926), all the way back to D. W. Griffith's *The Birth of a Nation* (1915), with its detailed restagings of the American Civil War and Lincoln's assassination, and *Intolerance* (1916), with its stunning re-creation / imagination of ancient Babylonian splendour.

In 1912, the year the *Titanic* sank, the biggest film spectacle was the Italian production *Quo Vadis?* (US release 1913), the highlight of which was the torching of ancient Rome by the mad emperor Nero. Back then, the Italians were famed for their film epics; they were the spectacle specialists. Their monumental *Cabiria* (1914), which envisioned ancient Rome's defeat of Carthage, was a box-office smash in America despite its previously unheard of three-hour running time. So great was its prestige that President Wilson screened it at the White House, the first movie ever to have been shown there. Another hit was *Gli Ultimi Giorni di Pompei* (two versions in 1908 and another two in 1913), from Edward Bulwer-Lytton's historical novel, *The Last Days of Pompeii* (1834), which in theatrical adaptation had long been a staple of the Victorian stage. One essential – if not the essential – element of such films was the re-creation of a vast historical catastrophe: the burning of Rome, the eruption of Vesuvius, a massacre of the innocents, a throwing of the Christians to the lions.

André Bazin remarked that such films bring out 'the Nero complex' in film audiences, who delight in watching massive destruction from the safety of their seats, as Nero is said to have enjoyed gazing upon the conflagration of his capital from the safety and comfort of his palace. Gilbert Adair adds, 'If Orson Welles was right, and the cinema is the most fabulous electric train set imaginable, then it would appear that its practitioners, like many an infant presented with a new train set, have had only one priority: to derail the train.'[45]

The bigger the apocalyptic event being described, the greater the public's demand for 'human interest' stories to personalize it. *Titanic* is no exception to this rule. A series of vignettes aboard the sinking ship give poignancy, drama or, indeed, melodrama to the sheer visual spectacle of the sight witnessed by Molly Brown, who stands in for the film audience, although she can only watch the proceedings from afar while we, by the nature of cinema, are permitted to see from close range as well.

All of the evacuation vignettes are archetypal in nature, encouraging viewers to approve or disapprove of the social constituencies being represented. In one vignette, Second Officer Lightoller, dark, intense, handsome, his face gaunt with what appears to be perennial anxiety, oversees the lowering of lifeboats that are only partially full. Mr Andrews,

A disaster pretty as a picture

designer of the *Titanic* who, as in *A Night to Remember*, has taken on the role of the managerial guilty conscience, puts a stop to this waste of life-saving space and orders Lightoller to fill the boats to capacity. Tommy Ryan leads the charge of the steerage passengers who have been locked below decks by over-zealous stewards. Cal Hockley grabs a stack of greenbacks from his safe and says, 'I make my own luck,' to which his man Lovejoy, smiling nefariously, draws back his jacket to reveal his nickel-plated handgun and replies, 'So do I.' The steerage passengers tear a bench from its moorings and use it to batter down a grating that has kept them out of the first-class gangways, and Tommy Ryan punches over a steward who protests this vandalizing of White Star Lines property. Lightoller threatens the surging steerage passengers with a gun: 'Get back, I say, or I'll shoot you all like dogs.' He then turns his back, takes a deep breath, and reveals to us, not them, that his gun isn't yet loaded. In effect, this 'human interest' disclosure places us, at least for the moment, on his side, not theirs.

In its own effort to forestall panic, the band plays insipid tea music on the upper deck while passengers scurry hither and yon like billiard balls scattered by a break. 'What's the use?' one of the band members sighs, 'Nobody's listening to us.' Replies the band leader, 'Well, they don't listen to us at dinner, either.' With that he adds a single word, *Orpheus*, and the band launches into Offenbach. This is one of the sweetest and most touching small moments in a large film. It has to do with modesty, self-effacement and commitment to one's art regardless of audience response. Providing something other than stiff-upper-lipism or any other heroic affectation, the vignette is flavoured by a bittersweet humility of the sort found in Jean Renoir masterpieces such as *The Crime of Monsieur Lange* (1936) and *The Rules of the Game* (1939), where unpretentious writers and musicians don't so much transcend the human condition as muddle through it with a spot of grace.

The choice of Offenbach is at once ironic and apt. Ironic, because Offenbach's 'can-can' from his 1858 operetta *Orpheus in the Underworld* is known everywhere as the musical emblem of carefree gaiety. Apt, because the Greek legend from which the operetta draws its name is the story of a musician who could tame wild beasts with his lyre-playing; here it is wild

passengers that the Orpheans are attempting to tame. Moreover, the
Thracian artist descends into Hades in a futile attempt to bring his
beloved Eurydice back from the dead. *Titanic*, like Eurydice, is headed for
Hades, and these musicians are not up to the job of bringing her back. In
story terms, Jack will play Orpheus to Rose's Eurydice, for when the ship
splits in half and the hull is sucked into the vortex, Rose will be plunged

Rose and Jack, racing against oblivion; *On the Waterfront*

into the depths and Jack will pull her out again, ultimately sacrificing his life for hers. Yet, too, is Orpheus thematically appropriate: in the frame story, Brock Lovett and his team attempt to reclaim the Eurydicean *Titanic* from the oceanic underworld. So, too, do Cameron and his crew attempt to raise the sunken ship and its ghosts from layers upon layers of historical memory and legend, bringing them back up, as it were, into the vivifying light of cinematic immediacy.

Myths, ancient or modern, are plausible only up to a point, but what really matters is whether or not they are able to quicken the pulse and fire the imagination. Much of *Titanic* is certainly mythic, if not nightmarish, in that regard. In one slow-motion action sequence that occurs later in the film, Jack and Rose race down a corridor with a tidal wall of water crashing behind them.[46] Is this realistic? No. Is it cinematic? Most emphatically. In *On the Waterfront* (1954), Marlon Brando and Eva Marie Saint find themselves in a similar predicament as they are chased down a narrow urban alley by a truck that barrels after them with murderous intent, and their escape through a side door at the last possible instant is similarly implausible but, never the less, truly thrilling.

As the scene continues, with the overhead electric lights flashing maniacally on and off and the music track pounding away with the brutal, jackhammer rhythms of an industrial or post-industrial wasteland (à la *Terminator*), the visual and auditory commotion of the race through the ship's labyrinth is dizzying. The scene climaxes when the lovers emerge from the mouth of the labryinth only to find themselves trapped by a locked gate. As the icy water stirs up against them, they spot a steward scurrying down a hallway toward a flight of stairs that is out of their reach. 'Wait, Sir, open the gate, please!' they beg of him as he sets foot on the stairs. He sizes up the situation, hesitates on behalf of his own safety, then mutters 'bloody hell' and comes down to help them. In his nervousness, he drops his ringful of keys into the depths of the pooling water. 'I'm sorry,' he cries, unable to give any more of himself before turning his back and fleeing for his life.

Jack dives into the water in search of the key (shades of the famous lost key scene in Hitchcock's 1951 thriller *Strangers on a Train*) and comes up with it as the water has left only inches of breathing space for him and Rose. 'Hurry, Jack. Hurry, Jack,' she implores again and again, her voice growing shriller and shriller with each repetition. Strobescent lighting, clanging, banging music, frantically paced editing and Rose's breathless, shrivelled, fear-throttled imprecation, 'Hurry, Jack,' lend the scene the frenzy of a primordial nightmare of drowning or suffocation. In 1950s America, there was a popular TV game show, 'Beat the Clock', in which contestants had to perform a series of deceptively simple mechanical actions before a large clock on the studio wall ticked down to zero. Jack's effort to insert the right key into the lock and open the gate before drowning is a 'Beat the Clock' moment from hell. He is everyone who has ever, in a bad dream, fumbled with a door lock while a brutal attacker bears down relentlessly.

Hell is no respecter of persons. It rears its hydra head everywhere. When Murdoch sees that Bruce Ismay has taken a place in one of the lifeboats, he stares with revulsion at the shame-faced shipping executive. Disgusted, as much with himself as with the company that has employed him, he issues the command, 'Take them down.' We hear *Orpheus* in the background, and, indeed, the Hades that Ismay and Murdoch, each in his own way, is being taken down to is an altogether different sort of hell from the one to which most of the hapless passengers have been consigned. The contrast is striking between the self-effacement of the band that stays at its post playing Offenbach and the literal self-effacement of Ismay, who

'Take them down'

cowers in the shadows, hoping not to be seen or recognized for his dereliction of duty.

Old-Time Melodrama

The next sequence brings together several strands of the story. The romantic triangle between Rose and the two men in her life arrives at climax and resolution. So, too, though less neatly, does the class-conflict triangle represented by Cal, Tommy Ryan and Mr Murdoch. In both cases, the conflicts and their respective resolutions are formulaic in nature but nonetheless compelling. This is because both types of stories – the triumph of romantic love over arranged marriage and the massacre of the innocents by the rich and greedy – are deeply embedded in modern (i.e. post-feudal) democratic cultures and continue to strike a responsive chord with readers, listeners or viewers so long as they are told with style and flare, as they most certainly are here.

The reason I say that the class-conflict triangle is less neatly resolved than the romantic one is that in the latter there is no question for the audience as to what's right and wrong. Clearly Rose belongs with Jack, not Cal, and nothing within the film leads the viewer to think otherwise. The class triangulation, for all its stereotyping, is not so easy to sort out. Clearly Cal is a pig, but he is not allowed to stand for all capitalists, as he would have in a Soviet motion picture of the 1920s such as Eisenstein's *Strike* (1924), where owners and industrialists are savaged indiscriminately by the film's satirical rhetoric. Unlike *Strike*, *Titanic* offers up for admiration several good and humane representatives of the ruling class – indeed, some might object that the Hollywood film is *too* fair-minded in its treatment of the ruling class. But it is equally benign in its treatment of the underclass passengers and, different from *A Night to Remember*, it does not make a point of insulting the common seamen.

It's in the social middle ground occupied by the professional managerial class, represented here by Andrews, Captain Smith and First Officer Murdoch, that the film achieves some of its best and most understatedly complex characterizations. The Murdoch sequence comprises one of the darkest vignettes in the film. It begins when

Murdoch flings back the wad of bills he had earlier accepted from Cal in return for an assured place in a lifeboat. It's clear that the officer despises himself for having allowed Ismay safe passage and can't stomach further complicity with the bosses. But neither can he give way to the panic of the mob. As the steerage passengers swarm around him and are about to surge into one of the few remaining lifeboats, Murdoch insists on order. Tommy Ryan shouts, 'Give us a chance to live, you limey bastards!' Murdoch fires his revolver twice in the air, but when a desperate man leaps out of the crowd, pushing Tommy along with him, Murdoch himself panics and shoots them both. Tommy falls dead. Murdoch turns to his fellow officers and salutes smartly. Then he puts the gun to his temple. Faster than he can pull the trigger, the camera cuts to an overhead vantage point. The jolting

Murdoch's suicide

switch in viewing angle, together with the clinical, almost abstract, starkness of the position from which we observe Murdoch's self-execution, causes us to flinch as his instantly lifeless body recoils from the bullet to the brain and flops unheroically off the deck into the water.

The romantic triangle is resolved at an earlier point, before the Murdoch sequence. As a lifeboat is being filled with women and children, both Cal and Jack tell Rose she must join them. Cal removes his coat and places it over Rose's shoulders to protect her from the cold. This seems uncharacteristically generous of him, and the viewer wonders if the film will go easier on Cal now, making him less of an ogre and even providing him with a touch of decency. It's doesn't take long, though, for the old one-dimensional Cal to reappear. Once Rose has been lowered away, he turns to Jack and lets him know that he has his own reserved spot in a lifeboat waiting for him on the other side of the ship. 'I always win, Jack,' he says with a smile. 'One way or another.'

But Jack focuses his attention instead on Rose as she is being lowered away. With the cardboard villain temporarily out of the picture, the sequence is left entirely to the two young lovers. A point-of-view shot from Rose's perspective shows a rocket bursting into light behind Jack's beatific face, and the effect is exactly the opposite of what occurred earlier when her face was bleached by the light of a flare. Here the effect is to grace Jack with a halo, indicative of her feelings about him.

Beatific

The distance widening between the two lovers, the cross-cutting of their close-ups is a familiar editing device from any number of old films in which lovers are torn apart as the train pulls out of the station, leaving one of them behind to watch helplessly as the other is propelled toward a different and separate destiny. This is also a basic motif of the *pas de deux* in classical dance and its permutations in the popular musicals of Broadway and Hollywood: in the plasticity of romantic longing, arms, legs, fingers, entire bodies stretch toward their vanishing counterparts as the music soars and achingly pleads. Similarly, in the love duets of tragic opera and its twentieth-century popular descendants, the male and female voices twist around the harmonic contours of one another as they slowly, reluctantly, pull apart.

Indeed, the very term 'melodrama' is of eighteenth-century coinage, referring originally to stage drama that was scored to music. This scene in *Titanic*, played without dialogue and comprised entirely of looks, gestures and a lyrical love theme, draws upon the longstanding tradition of romantic melodrama that found form in the nineteenth century in ballet and opera as well as in the potboilers of the theatrical stage. The photographic sheen and fizz, together with the pop-idol looks of Leonardo DiCaprio, give the scene a superficial resemblance to the MTV music videos of today, but its truer lineage is to the luminous melodramas of the silent era, where in visual masterpieces such as Griffith's *Orphans of the Storm* (1922), Borzage's *Seventh Heaven* (1927) and Murnau's *Sunrise* (1927), the parting of lovers (or, in the case of *Orphans*, siblings) is portrayed with sublimely outsized emotion.

The light from the flare not only hallows Jack, it also, when crossing Rose's face, signals another dawning recognition, this being that she can't leave him behind. She hurls herself out of the lifeboat as it passes the A deck. She has chosen to return to the sinking ship to survive or die with the man she loves. As she races into the interior to find him, he sprints down to A deck, the music surging with romantic ardour. Verdi and Puccini would have understood; so too would Griffith, Borzage and Murnau. The lovers meet at the bottom of the Grand Staircase. This, like the bow railing and the aft railing, is another of the sites on the ship that gains symbolic resonance through repetition. By their very nature staircases have often served a dramatic function as metaphors for upward and downward social mobility (as in the mid-1970s British television serial *Upstairs, Downstairs*), and film-makers of Hollywood's Golden Age, such as Max Ophuls, Douglas Sirk and William Wyler, made great use of them for their ability to convey class distinction, or other types of hierarchical difference, through 'cine-architecture'. When Rhett Butler carries Scarlett O'Hara upstairs in his arms towards the end of *Gone With The Wind*, the majestic staircase beneath his feet surrenders to, and even abets, his assertion of mastery over the mistress of the mansion, even as the entrepreneurial New South that Rhett embodies rises to dominance over Scarlett's vanquished Old South. One has only to think of Hitchcock's almost obsessive reliance on staircases as venues for murder, intrigue and Oedipal nightmare in movies such as *Suspicion* (1941), *Spellbound* (1945), *Notorious* (1946), *Vertigo* (1958) and *Psycho* (1959) to understand that, for the best of film directors, it can rarely be said that a staircase is sometimes only a staircase.

As Rose and Jack embrace ecstatically, he upbraids her: 'Rose, you're so stupid. Why did you do that, huh? You're so stupid, Rose.' All the while he's covering her with kisses. Her reply nails him with his own words: 'You jump, I jump, right?' They're in this together, live or die. How much better, she is saying, to die together than to live apart. In a word, *Liebestod*. Love in death. In Wagner's great music drama of 1859, *Tristan and Isolde*, a medieval princess, Isolde, is sent by sea to wed a man she

A modern Tristan and Isolde

does not love. Along the way she falls tumultuously in love with the young knight who escorts her, Tristan, and he with she. Closing themselves off from the crass outer world, they pledge endless, undying, oceanic love – a *Liebestod*.

More than a century's worth of music critics and moral custodians alike have condemned Wagner for the shimmering seductiveness with which he rendered erotic rapture as a narcoticizing and totally asocial force of nature, but there you have it, it has resurfaced countless times in both the high and the low arts of the twentieth century, from Mahler, Strauss and Schoenberg to romance fiction, teen rock and the Hollywood dream machine. Bernard Herrmann went so far as to base his score for *Vertigo* on *Tristan*, for Wagner's restless, relentless, endlessly shifting harmonies, above all other instances of Western music, embody the implacable yearnings of solipsistic desire. (Hitchcock, of course, was a strict moralist and, in that sense, an anti-Wagnerian. Films such as *Vertigo* and *Psycho* are cautionary tales that describe the nightmarish effects of libidinal release, and his characters who yield to their own sexualized urgings destroy not only themselves but others who enter their orbit.) As Michael Tanner has written about *Tristan*, 'It is a work of anti-civilization, and its appeal, the violent and profound effect it has upon us, is intimately bound up with that.'[47]

The relevance of *Tristan* to *Titanic* is that the film translates the opera's ideology of romantic passion, its pagan creed of erotic attachment transcending life and death, into terms easily accessible to late twentieth-century consumers. This ideology is most explicitly conveyed by the lyrics of 'My Heart Will Go On', the Oscar- and Grammy-winning hit song from the film that topped pop charts for months and sold millions of copies worldwide.[48] Addressing her absent (or, more specifically, deceased) lover, the singer declares, 'Every night in my dreams I see you, I feel you, / That is how I know you go on. / Far across the distance and spaces between us / You have come to show you go on. / Near, far, wherever you are, / I believe that the heart does go on.'

This is *Tristan* for the masses. Wagner himself had hopes that *Tristan* would appeal to the masses, but the opera proved far too strange and demanding, not to mention morally decadent, to provide him with the commercial success he was bent upon achieving. *Tristan*'s sensibility is still too extreme and rarefied to give it mass appeal, but its underlying doctrine of reckless romantic self-gratification – crudely put, 'Do your own thing,' 'Let nothing stand in your way,' 'Go for it,' 'Just do it!' – is considerably more relevant and socially acceptable now than it was a century and a half ago. As Woody Allen explained in 1992 as to why he left his lover of many years for her adopted daughter, 'The heart wants what it wants; there's no logic to those things.' [49] In other words, romantic passion, sheer personal desire, trumps social or public responsibility. This is the essence of Wagnerism and, as noted above, the other forms of Antinomianism that are deeply woven into the film. (Wagnerism has also come to refer to artistic giganticism, or art-music-drama spectacle of enormous length and scale, which aptly characterizes the film *Titanic* as well.)

But if Rose is determined to throw over propriety in her zeal to fulfil personal desire, the man she is reacting against, Cal, is even more self-absorbed. Her desire, though culturally descended from Isolde's, is shown to be healthy. It affirms not only herself and Jack but others around them (for instance, the stranded little boy they attempt to rescue in a couple of scenes hence). Cal's desire, on the other hand, has no redeeming or counter-balancing features. Nor is it even romantic. It is crassly sexual and narcissistic, and when he reaches the limits of his ability to cope with frustration, this tormented desire goes veering out of control. He takes off after the romantic pair through the now-flooded first-class dining salon, waving his gun at them wildly and firing high-calibre bullets that explode into the waist-high water through which they tread, thus graphically indicating the nearness of his misses. Later, the contrast between Rose's benevolent obedience to her inner dictates and Cal's malevolent obedience to his is heightened when he, too, scoops up an abandoned child, but only, we quickly learn, as a subterfuge to get himself into a lifeboat.

No, it is not Cal who embodies the film's counter-voice to its romantic anthem of following your own personal impulses (i.e. 'the heart') without paying heed to the established social order. Instead, this voice is offered up by a chorus of secondary characters, all of whom significantly

reappear at this crucial point in the story. Forlorn Mr Andrews stares at a clock on a mantelpiece and offers Rose his life preserver. Remorseful about his own role in the disaster, he awaits death like a Roman senator who knows he has failed the republic and accepts the punishment he feels he deserves. Captain Smith is similarly stoical. Making no effort to save himself, he stands with calm resignation at the bridge of the ship, facing the rising flood that is about to implode upon him. Benjamin Guggenheim, dressed in his finest evening apparel as he awaits the dark lady, refuses the offer of a life vest but asks instead for a brandy. And Murdoch, though he faltered by taking a bribe, stands at the barricades, resisting the onslaught of the capitalist and the proletarian alike, until he concludes he can do no more. These might be called counter-Wagnerian moments, in the sense that they epitomize, sympathetically at that, a classical conception of decorum, restraint and acceptance of one's pre-determined position in the social order and all that that entails.

Most counter-Wagnerian of all, in this sense of the term, is the lovely small scene in which the band finishes its last number, and the leader dismisses the musicians with thanks. As they disperse, he picks up his violin and begins a solo. Hearing this, the others return to join him in a plaintive melody, as all around them crashes a human storm of chaos and social disorder. This incident also figured prominently in *A Night to Remember*. It culminated with the cellist taking a seat on deck and playing a solo rendition of 'Nearer, My God, to Thee' as he sang the lyrics in a

Mr Andrews' stoic resignation

steady tenor, the camera focused in on his solemn performance. In *Titanic*, however, the incident opens the door to a montage sequence of genuine power and beauty. The elegiac tones of the hymn play over a series of cuts from the captain alone on the bridge to Andrews by the fireplace clock to an elderly couple (Ida and Isidor Straus) snuggled together in fear and resignation on a narrow bed to a young Irish mother in steerage telling a bedtime tale to her two beguiled children to Monet's water lillies and Degas's dancers floating upward together from the bottom of Rose's now submerged stateroom. Then, suddenly, back to the noise and confusion of the mobs on deck and in the jammed lifeboats, but still with the overlay of music, so measured and mournful in ironic contrast to the frenzy. The band leader thanks the other members: 'Gentlemen, it has been a privilege playing with you tonight.'

This is the moment before the apocalypse. When this sequence comes to an end, the final unleashing of hell begins. Guggenheim, clasping his snifter of brandy, opens his eyes wide in an expression of horror that all his deepest convictions and training in gentlemanly deportment cannot hide, Andrews is swept away, and Captain Smith, from his post at the bridge, is crushed in an instant as tidal waves of incoming sea demolish not only him but the venerable tradition of British naval rectitude and stewardship that he, by his appointed role, represents.

We're back to Wagner again, but this time *Tristan* is not the relevant reference, instead it's *Götterdämmerung* – the Twilight of the Gods. At the

'Gentlemen, it has been a privilege playing with you tonight'

end of Wagner's great opera of 1874, itself the culmination of the four-part *Ring of the Niebelungen*, the Rhine overflows and Valhalla, the home of the gods, is consumed by flood and flame. Only the Rhinemaidens, the mythological spirits of the all-encompassing water, survive the catastrophe. They return to their native depths having recovered for themselves the stolen Ring of Gold that, like *Titanic*'s Heart of the Ocean, set the whole long narrative cycle in motion.

From Bayreuth to Coney Island

Over the many years during which Wagner was writing the *Ring* cycle, he came to the realization that no opera house in Europe was equipped to stage the epic spectacle he envisioned. He needed to invent a new type of theatre that would allow for sonorous waves of singing and playing to wash over audiences while their eyes were transfixed by pinpoint lighting and sweeping vistas. His goal was what aesthetic philosophers have called 'synaesthesia', or the synthesizing of multiple aesthetic experiences into a single unity of sight and sound, music and drama. Assisted by large loans from his patron, King Ludwig of Bavaria, Wagner built the synaesthetic auditorium of his dreams, the Bayreuth Festspielhaus. Completed in 1874, this structure might be thought of as a prototype movie theatre engineered more than a generation before the birth of the cinema, two generations before the construction of the great picture palaces of the 1920s, and more than a century before the birth of the modern Dolby-equipped multiplex, without which major synaesthetic events like *Titanic* could not have come to fruition.

Although the first performance of the *Ring* was jubilantly staged in Bayreuth to a glittering audience of crowned heads and famous composers, the cost of the production was so exorbitant (of *Titanic*-like proportions, by the standards of the day) that Wagner amassed an enormous personal debt that it took him years to offset. Eventually the festspielhaus grew in fame and acclaim, but it never even approached in popular appeal the success of a very different synaesthesic environment that was developing on the East Coast of the US in the same years in a beachfront area of New York City known as Coney Island.

Coney Island – Shooting the Chutes at Luna Park (1903, UPI/Corbis)

Coney Island's 'Luna Park' was America's first great amusement resort. Modelled upon the famous Midway of the 1893 Chicago World's Fair, Luna Park immersed visitors in myriad sights, sounds, tastes and smells, all beckoning simultaneously to be sampled, paid for and enjoyed. The visitor was encouraged to lose him or herself in the overwhelming plenitude of spectacle and sensation. Pseudo-educational or anthropological displays jostled for space with Barnumesque freak shows, hedonism was not only rampant but *de rigeur*, and, over the years, a technology of controlled or illusionistic danger was put into operation for a crowd of thrill-seekers who wished to taste in their mouths and guts the tartness of fear before washing it all away with a cold glass of lemonade, sarsaparilla or beer.[50]

'Fire and Flames' was a popular Luna Park exhibition in which a wooden house, specially built for the occasion, was set afire each night only to be saved by a fire crew that rushed to the scene and doused the flames. 'Helter Skelter' and 'Flip Flap' were turn-of-the-century thrill machines. By the 1910s, the mammoth Coney Island roller coaster, renowned throughout the world, transported paying customers up a narrow-gauge railway to staggering heights before plunging them down again with a dizzying, even nauseating, velocity. An early developer of Luna Park explained that visitors came to the resort looking for something 'different from ordinary experience. What is presented to them must have life, action, motion, sensation, surprise, shock, swiftness or else comedy.'[51]

Titanic has now reached the Luna Park stage. The film becomes a cinematic amusement park – or, as suggested in the heading above, Bayreuth meets Coney Island. As the bow of the liner plunges under the water, its stern levers upward into the night. Crowds frantically rush up deck while other passengers spill over the railings into the sea. Cal, in a lifeboat, bats away a swimmer who futilely attempts to climb aboard (virtually the same incident as in *A Night to Remember*, but with a capitalist rather than a sailor committing the deed). Fabrizio, in the water, is buried beneath a massive smokestack, which topples over on him and numerous other hapless victims. Jack and Rose proceed up an outer gangway behind an elderly man who is reciting the 23rd Psalm. When the man comes to the line 'Yea, though I walk through the valley of the shadow of death,'

Jack quips, 'You wanna walk a little faster through that valley there?' We, in our sound-, light- and temperature-controlled movie theatre, are given to enjoy (if enjoy is the right word) something that is indeed altogether 'different from ordinary experience' and full of 'life, action, motion, sensation, surprise, shock, swiftness' – and even, if feebly, given the quality of Jack's zingers, 'comedy'.

Nowhere is the film's Coney Islandization of experience more palpable than in the sequence of shots that follows Jack's remark. First, we look beyond John Jacob Astor as the glass dome above the grand staircase collapses beneath a crushing deluge. Then we look down to see dozens of passengers swept hither and yon by the frothing torrents. And, finally, in a moment of pure action, motion, sensation, surprise, shock and swiftness, we hurl backward along with the camera through a flooding corridor at breakneck speed, experiencing the velocity and pressure of the water as it bursts forward into our viewing space as though cannonading out of a fire hose. While this is happening, cabin doors snap open from their hinges and fly violently across the screen.

The young lovers reach the aft railing. The irony is not lost on Rose, who remarks, 'Jack, this is where we first met.' The love music soars. Nearby, a priest prays aloud, trembling. Inside the liner, a female corpse swathed in a white ball gown floats upward like an angel or an apparition. Fancy dishes slide out of their shelves in the ship's pantry, indicating the dramatic pitch of the incline. Molly Brown, looking on from afar, gasps in horror at the terrible

Passengers sliding down the deck

spectacle of the great ocean liner splitting in half (as we were made to understand that it would from the computer display provided for us two and a half hours ago). Bruce Ismay, the Judas of the story, cannot bring himself to look at the crucifixion of the innocents that he has wrought. The ship goes dark as the electric power fails. This literal darkness bespeaks the moral darkness of the corporate machinery blamed for the disaster.

The most stupendous of the movie's special effects is presently unveiled as the stern, now split loose, cantilevers upward past 45 degrees then past 60, flinging off everyone without a railing or post to grasp. People skid helter-skelter down the poop deck screaming and flailing, unable to break their free fall.[52] Jack climbs over the stern railing and pulls Rose to him in the exact opposite direction of his rescue of her two nights earlier. When the stern reaches the full 90 degrees, they cling white-knuckled to the aft railing as fellow passengers tumble down, down, down vertiginous heights to the vexed sea below, crashing and bumping along the way into one another or into the hardware of the ship – in a particularly grotesque instance, into one of its mammoth propeller blades. Seeing all of this from afar, as from Molly Brown's vantage point, is like watching others screaming in terror on a giant amusement park ride; you're in sympathy with them, but relieved not to be in their boat. Seeing it from directly on top of the action, however, is almost equivalent to going on the terrifying ride itself.

The apex of the thrill machine

As the camera swings out over and above the aft railing in a gruesome reprise of the aerial shots that swooned above the bow railing when the two lovers embraced at sunset the previous evening, the verticality of the fifteen-story drop is staggering, and the effect is visceral, as on an amusement park ride when it reaches its apex for one perilous, heart-stopping moment before plunging into the abyss.[53]

Into the Water, Finally

So Rose makes it into the water after all, some two hours of screen time after her contemplated suicide. As before, Jack is with her. This time he cannot rescue her, inasmuch as the ship itself is going under.

As planned, they jump clear of the leviathan. 'Do not let go of my hand,' he had warned her before they went under. His counsel is, of course, not only practical but thematic: not letting go of the beloved, as we have noted, is the film's overriding romantic ethos (and the source, one must surmise, of so much of its popular appeal).

Yet deep beneath the water Rose does let go, and when she comes to the surface, Jack is gone. She calls for him, but he doesn't answer. She calls again. In one of the great shots of the film, the camera pulls back from a close-up of her forlorn face to an overhead wide angle view of an endless blue-black seascape littered with hundreds of flailing and thrashing bodies. In film history terms, it's the equivalent of the memorable shot in *Gone With the Wind* when Scarlett enters the main square of Atlanta after the Yankees have swept through and the camera pulls back and back and back to show the enormity of the suffering and destruction all around her. Only in cinema can this sort of effect be achieved – not in painting or photography, literature or drama. Rose's terrifying aloneness is registered in a progressive visual revelation of the equal aloneness of hundreds of other distraught victims all around her. This is the one of the grimmest and most terrifying revelations of all.

A man tries to save himself by climbing up on Rose's shoulders, forcing her head under. This is the signal for Jack to reappear. He throws off the intruder. 'Swim, Rose,' he commands his gasping lover. 'I need you to swim.'

Later, a wooden door or section of panelling floats by them. There's only room on it for one. Rose sprawls across it in exhaustion while Jack clings to it and treads icy water. Stars fill the vaulted night sky. When the lovers speak, vapour rises from their mouths. They shiver from the cold.

Freezing in the water

Nearby, a ship's officer in a life vest blows hard upon his whistle. 'The boats are coming back for us, Rose,' Jack assures her.

Heeding the distant whistle, Molly Brown urges her fellow passengers to turn the lifeboat back in the direction of the survivors in the water, but the passengers, shamefaced, are unable to provide either physical or moral support, and the seaman in charge of the vessel firmly reprimands her, 'There'll be one less [survivor] on this boat if you don't shut that hole in your face.' Elsewhere, however, Fifth Officer Lowe decides to send back a rescue boat. This requires dispersing the passengers out of his boat into the others, and that will take time. The survivors in the freezing water don't have much at their disposal.

A dissolve shows that an unspecified period has elapsed. The dissolve is to the officer who was blowing the whistle. He now bobs in the water like a slab of ice. Nearby, Jack is literally freezing to death. Frost covers his hair. His teeth chattering, his lips emitting a frigid vapour, he makes one of his feeble little jokes: 'I don't know about you,' he remarks to the nearly comatose Rose, 'but I intend to write a strongly worded letter to the White Star Line about all of this.'

This rouses something in her. 'I love you, Jack,' she manages to say.

'Don't you do that' he snaps back. 'Don't say your goodbyes. Not yet, do you understand me?'

Her reply, 'I can't feel my body,' elicits from him the declaration that embodies the nineteenth-century romantic and anti-naturalist view of destiny that underpins the film: 'Winning that ticket, Rose, was the best thing that ever happened to me. It brought me to you.' True love trumps disaster, and life lived fully removes death of its sting.

In 'The Open Boat' (1899), Stephen Crane's classic tale of four survivors of a shipwreck cast adrift in an unprotected dinghy in freezing temperatures, the appalling indifference of the universe rankles them. 'When it occurs to a man that nature does not regard him as important, and that she feels she would not maim the universe by disposing of him, he at first wishes to throw bricks at the temple, and he hates deeply the fact that there are no bricks and no temples.'[54] Jack doesn't rage against nature, nor, despite his mild joke, does he rage against the corporate profiteering that placed him in his present predicament. Instead, with a stoic acceptance of fate that Crane would have found as absurd as fate itself, he stays his course as Rose's mentor in the art of living. 'Promise me you'll survive,' he says to her, his teeth achatter. 'That you won't give up … no matter what happens … no matter how hopeless … promise me now, Rose, and never let go of that promise.'

Throughout the film he has urged her to fight stultification. And now death.

'Never let go,' he insists.

'I will never let go, Jack. I'll never let go.'

Their hands are entwined. He presses his frozen lips against her fingers.

A Floating Necropolis

Lowe's rescue boat approaches out of the darkness. The blade-faced officer sweeps a handheld electric beam over the human detritus that litters the black surface of the sea. What is shown is a ghastly sight, acres of frozen bodies and upturned faces assembled quietly in the water. The Greek term *necropolis*, or city of the dead, seems more apt here than graveyard, for this is not a cemetary of isolated bodies encased in coffins and buried from sight, but a community of fully dressed men, women and children who, supported by their flotation belts, are positioned upright in the water and crowded together as if on a public conveyance or at a public event, say, a motion picture show. The light beam picks out horrific details – for example, a mother in white, her face ghastly and drawn, cradling a dead infant – but it is the massiveness of the death, its apparent endlessness, that is so overwhelming and, to the film viewer, all too unnervingly familiar.

For we live in an era haunted by mass death. This is only to be expected in the age of mass society. Ships have sunk for thousands of years, but they were never the size of the *Titanic* and thus could not lay claim to having caused so many deaths all at once. In the summer of 1996, a passenger airliner, TWA 800, went down over the Atlantic in a ball of fire, strewing the remains of hundreds of human bodies across the face of the sea. Two summers later, a Swiss Air jet crashed off the coast of Nova Scotia, again littering the sea with hundreds of grossly disfigured human remnants. Bracketed in time by these two real-world catastrophes, the 1997 film *Titanic*, with its excruciating depiction of modern tourist leisure transformed into modern mass death, cuts right to the nerve for audiences who eagerly participate in the one phenomenon and, in their heart of hearts, dread that they may also end up participating in the other.

Commentators on *Titanic* have likened it to the popular disaster films of the 1970s – *Airport* (1970), *The Poseidon Adventure* (1972), *The Towering Inferno* (1974) and *Earthquake* (1974) – but in none of those films was mass death envisioned as graphically, convincingly and seriously as here. Moreover, in those films, the hero was virtually assured of survival, no matter how perilous the situation: audiences knew full well that there was no way that box-office favourites such as Dean Martin, Gene Hackman, Paul Newman and Robert Redford would fail to come out of their respective disasters alive. Many viewers of *Titanic* probably expected the same rule to hold true for Leonardo DiCaprio.

As noted earlier, the cinema has long had a penchant for depicting catastrophes of mass destruction. Around the same time that movies took on this role, Coney Island showmen staged recreations of famous disasters such as 'The Fall of Pompeii', Pennsylvania's Johnstown Flood of 1889 and Texas's Galveston Flood of 1900. As John Kasson, the historian of Coney Island, explains,

In its very horror, disaster conferred a kind of transcendent meaning to its victims' lives, transforming commonplace routine into the extraordinary. Sensationalized re-creations of such disasters gave a vicarious sense of this transcendence to their audience – with of course the inestimable advantage of allowing them to emerge from the performance unharmed.[55]

Long before the advent of either cinema or Coney Island, nineteenth-century artists satisfied (as well as helped create) the public appetite for vicarious participation in disaster and its transcendence. John Martin's *The Fall of Babylon* (1831), Karl Briullov's enormous, movie-screen size

(15 by 21 feet) *Last Day of Pompeii* (1830–3), Thomas Cole's *The Course of Empire: Destruction* (1836) and J. M. W. Turner's *The Slave Ship* (1840) all revelled in death, mayhem and destruction, providing early nineteenth-century viewing audiences with titillating, if morally instructive, depictions of carnage. The masterpiece of the genre was Théodore Géricault's massive *Raft of the Medusa* (1818), based on a horrendous maritime disaster that had occurred two years earlier.

With its turbulent skies, roiling waves and pyramidally massed concantenation of naked limbs and anguished faces, Géricault's painting offended academic and journalistic critics of the time who deemed it crude and obvious. Unperturbed, the young French artist rolled up the canvas and took it on the road to London and Dublin, where it stirred audiences and proved an enormous commercial success. *Raft of the Medusa* invoked what was to become a standard theme of nineteenth-century Romanticism, the distressed vessel on troubled waters as a symbol of the modern state – or in other instances the individual soul – on its perilous journey. Walt Whitman's memorial lament for Lincoln at the conclusion of American Civil War is a famous version of this trope: 'O Captain! my Captain! our fearful trip is done, / The ship has weather'd every rack, the prize we sought / is won.'[56] The staying power of the ship-at-sea metaphor and its variations continues unabated today, as seen, for example, on the cover illustration of a globally distributed religious magazine that shows a father anxiously paddling a lifeboat on a stormy sea while his wife and children clutch at the ropes and the caption reads: 'The Family Under Threat – Will It Survive?'[57]

As Lowe's boat makes its way slowly through the frozen bodies that cover the surface of the sea like water lillies on a pond, he urges the rowers not to strike the dead with their oars. Filmed from a low angle, peering up at the boat and the starry sky beyond, this sequence of shots resembles the work of the nineteenth-century New England artist Winslow Homer, who, in oil paintings such as *Fog Warning* (1885) and *The Herring Net* (1885), produced a remarkable series of images of rugged fishermen and sailors contending with the sea for its bounty. As in Homer's paintings, here too does the elemental encounter of sailor and sea evoke primal emotions in the viewer.

A dissolve returns the focus to Rose on the floating door with Jack beside her in the water. She's absently singing, in a husky, cracked, almost inaudible voice, the words to a then-popular song that Jack sang to her earlier, 'Come with me, Josephine, in my flying machine.' The shouts of the rescuer arrive with a distant and distorted sound, as though a delusion. Jack's eyes are closed, his face quiet and reposed. She still grips his manacled hand. She whispers his name, and when he doesn't respond, she whispers it again, more urgently. His face is alabaster, like that of a beautiful, androgynous stone angel. He has frozen to death.

Again comes the eerily distorted, high-pitched voice of Lowe as he calls out for survivors. The rescuers pass nearby, not realizing that the young woman on the door is still alive. 'Jack! There's a boat, Jack,' she says, her cracked voice hardly more than a squeak. The mournful Gaelic lament from the opening of the film fills the soundtrack. The camera closes in on Rose, the vapour rising from her mouth, as she cries out

Théodore Géricault, *The Raft of the Medusa* (Musée du Louvre/AKG)

'Come back! Come back! Come back!' But her voice is too weak; it barely travels beyond her lips, as in a nightmare when the sleeper's desperate cries for help are choked inside. Passing into the distance, Lowe calls out, 'Can anyone hear me?'

Rose breaks her hand free of Jack's. 'I'll never let go, I promise,' she swears as she lets go in order to honour her promise not to let go. His corpse falls away into the deep. When he has disappeared from sight, she rolls off the door into the water. But not in the manner of a Juliet or Isolde yielding herself to the death that has claimed her lover. Instead she

Trawling for survivors; Winslow Homer, *The Herring Net* (Art Institute of Chicago)

THE **WATCHTOWER**
ANNOUNCING JEHOVAH'S KINGDOM

APRIL 1, 1998

**The Family
Under Threat
Will It Survive?**

thrashes through the water to the dead man with the whistle. Taking it from him, she thrusts it between her lips and blows a shrill, shrieking signal. At first it's not very loud, not nearly loud enough, but she keeps on blowing, each time louder and with greater force. We hear Lowe call to his men to come about, and still the whistle shrieks and shrieks and shrieks.

An electric beam cuts across Rose's face. She is haggard, wizened, a fright. No beautiful Hollywood starlet or fashionable society girl, Rose. Instead she looks like hell. Exactly what you would expect of someone who has been to that place and hasn't yet left it behind.

Salvage / Salvation

The camera cuts to a close-up of Rose's eyes – but they're the eyes of old Rose. 'Fifteen hundred people went into the sea when *Titanic* sank from under us,' she explains. 'Six were saved from the water, myself included.'

Her commentary, which calls to mind Robert Shaw's grim speech in *Jaws* (1975) about the World War II torpedoing of an eleven-hundred-man transport ship in shark-infested waters, begins the wind-down of the movie. The Jack-and-Rose narrative has essentially ended, and all that is needed now is to tie up loose ends. This is accomplished with considerable narrative skill.

The crew on the salvage ship are lined up in front of Rose, again like a row of audience members in a movie house. It's obvious that they have been moved by her tale – even Lewis, the lewd and crude techno-geek, is stained with a tear. A traditional device of melodrama is to show

The Watchtower, 1 April 1998: a familiar metaphor

characters within the fictive world of the story responding in an emotional fashion that models for the audience outside the story the manner in which they are to react – recoil with terror, laugh with delight, weep with pity and so forth. In this case, however, if *Titanic*'s audiences have not already bubbled over at Rose's story, no amount of on-screen prompting is going to elicit that response now. Still, the cutaway to Rose's on-board audience is appropriate inasmuch as it rhetorically supports the truth-claims made at the start of the film: personal (and feminine) ways of knowing are superior to impersonal, scientific and crudely masculine ones. It is shortly after this that Brock confides to Rose's winsome granddaughter that his three years of striving to salvage the Heart of the Ocean had failed to succeed in salvaging, as it were, the warm human heart for which the chilly diamond is but a poor substitute.

Back into her story, Rose speaks of the survivors who had to wait 'for an absolution that would never come'. Dissolves take us first to a bleak image of Ismay isolated in the darkness of approaching dawn and then to other survivors: Cal, Molly, Mother and Rose herself, supine and covered over by a woollen blanket and lit in a sickly greenish way by a rescue flare somewhere overhead.

The voice-over recounts coming aboard the *Carpathia*, where segregation by social class remained strictly in force. Rose, looking now like a poor immigrant, wears her woollen blanket over her head as Cal prowls the steerage section of the steamer in search of his fiancée. Says the

The steerage of the *Carpathia*

Photographic antecedents: Alfred Stieglitz, *The Steerage* (courtesy George Eastman House)

Lewis Hine, *Young Russian Jewess at Ellis Island* (courtesy George Eastman House)

ship's officer by his side, 'Sir, I don't think you'll find any of your people down here – it's all steerage.' Rose hears this, and by rejecting the opportunity to come forward and identify herself, shows how completely her class allegiance has shifted. When Jack first spotted Rose on the *Titanic*, he gazed up at her from steerage until Cal came to her side and led her away; this scene, then, is the symmetrical reversal of that.

The voice-over closes out Cal's role in the narrative. 'That's the last I ever saw him. He married, of course, and inherited his millions. But the crash of '29 hit his interests hard and he put a pistol in his mouth that year. Or so I read.'

Visually, Cameron alludes to two of the most influential images in the history of American still photography, Lewis Hine's *Young Russian Jewess at Ellis Island* (1905) and Alfred Stieglitz's *The Steerage* (1907). The latter photograph, with its striking visual contrasts, not so much between upper and lower social classes (a subject of little concern to Stieglitz) as between shapes, textures and tones, elicited the praise of none other than Pablo Picasso at the time he was completing *Demoiselles d'Avignon*, the avant-garde painting that Rose supposedly brings aboard *Titanic*. Even in its closing dramatic resolution, *Titanic* maintains its dedication to, or impish delight in, what might be called inter-art intertextuality, casting off a multitude of allusions as it goes.

In the following brief scene, the Statue of Liberty rises high in the background of the night as a hard rain drives down on Rose and her fellow

A new class identity

passengers in steeerage. A steward approaches. 'Can I take your name, please, love?' he inquires. Rose looks up when she answers. She speaks the very last words that she will say in the film. 'Dawson. Rose Dawson.' The love theme swells achingly on the music track. Eyes that have had a moment to dry are prompted to spring back into wetness.

Several things are accomplished here. A plot consideration is satisfied. Because there is no record of a 'Rose Dawson' having been aboard the *Titanic*, we are given to understand why armies of zealous *Titanic* researchers never tracked down this particular survivor, as they have all the others: someone else did survive, but because she assumed another name, another identity, without telling anyone, she has gone unrecorded. The implication is that this story could be true, after all, and was simply never known before now.

Second, Rose's assumption of Jack's last name completes the transference of class allegiance that has been an underlying subject of the film. By taking his name as her own, she finishes the business she had begun much earlier of rejecting Cal's social class and the particular brand of patriarchical dominance with which she associated it. Instead she has amalgamated herself with what the film has portrayed as the red-blooded, foot-stomping, salt-of-the-earth egalitarian international working class – the class from which millions upon millions of Americans of today, through their grandparents and great-grandparents, presumably have sprung. (It is much easier for middle-class Americans to sentimentalize the working class of former rather than current generations.)

The third and most obvious function of Rose's identification of herself as Rose Dawson is to complete the romantic trajectory of their love story. It symbolizes her pledge never to let go. It is poignant and chokingly ironic – he has vanished into the sea without a trace, and this, the name she has taken for herself, is all she has left of him.

But it is not all that she has left. For she reaches into the pocket of the man's overcoat she is wearing – Cal's – and, with a quizzical expression on her face, pulls out an object within. It is the Heart of the Ocean. Only now are we likely to recall that after Cal had given up his murderous pursuit of Jack and Rose with Lovejoy's revolver, he had burst into sudden laughter.

When Lovejoy asked what could possibly be so funny, Cal replied: 'I put the diamond in the coat. And I put the coat on her!'

Cut to old Rose on the salvage ship. On the video monitor behind her head is a view of the underwater wreckage: specifically, of the ship's bow railing. 'He saved me – in every way that a person can be saved. I don't even have a picture of him,' she says of Jack. 'He exists now only in my memory.'

A close-up of Rose gives way to a full-screen view of the railing itself as the submersible pulls away from the wreckage. This underwater view then fades to black.

Night aboard the salvage ship. Brock, paired with Rose's granddaughter, gives his speech about his misguided three-year obsession with the *Titanic*. His expression of frustration and insight is followed by a cut to a close-up view of the dark, rhythmic waves of the sea – the same 'timeless' view provided at the very opening of the film. Cut again to the deck of the salvage ship, presumably later that night. Elderly Rose, backlit and clad in her white nightgown like an apparition, her long white hair loose about her shoulders, treads barefoot upon the aft deck. The Gaelic music with the ethereal female voice adds to the haunting dimension of the moment. As Rose climbs onto the aft railing, an insert close-up reveals her toenails to be painted red – a sign of the vivacious and flirtatious 17-year-old who still inhabits her, but also a reminder of the identical close-up of the red satin shoes that she was wearing on the night that she climbed *Titanic*'s aft railing to dispose of herself.

She opens her hand. There, nestled in her palm, is the Heart of the Ocean. Cut to a high-angled shot of Rose on Ellis Island discovering the diamond in her pocket. Cut back to old Rose, eighty-four years later. She gasps with a thrill or sense of unburdenment as she flings it into the sea. It swirls down, presumably toward Jack, with a flourish.

Dissolve to Rose's night table. At last the camera reveals the contents of the various framed photographs that we had seen her neatly arrange on the table when she arrived on the ship. The camera pans slowly past them: Rose as an aviatrix of the early 1930s, Rose lounging glamorously as a fashionable movie diva, Rose standing proudly beside a

giant deep-water fish she has caught, Rose riding a horse in the surf with the Santa Monica roller coaster in the distance – in this instance, doing on her own what she and Jack had once planned to do together. A full and active life, is the suggestion here; the life that he urged her – and taught her – to live.

At the end of the assemblage of photographs is Rose herself, reposed in sleep, or maybe even death. The movie doesn't tell us which is the case. Instead, it dissolves from this image back to an image of the underwater wreckage. The eerie, beautiful singing rises and the camera moves rapidly and gracefully along the outer deck and onto an inner deck. The drab grey-green underwater colours transform before our eyes into the rich and vivid browns of an elegant, newly panelled corridor. So many corridor shots in this film; this one is the last. Still the camera swoops

The past recovered; Rose as horsewoman

along until it is inside and comes to a glass-windowed doorway, where a smiling steward is there to greet it – or, as we now discern, to greet Rose, whose subjective point of view we have assumed.

The doors open for us / Rose, and inside, the great lobby of the *Titanic* is full of light and life again, perfectly intact. Still the camera continues to move forward, rapturously, as we / Rose are met by the passengers of the *Titanic* brought back to life, happy ghosts as it were, resurrected and redeemed. With the significant exception of Cal, Lovejoy and Ismay, all are there to greet her. They beam with joy and acceptance. The camera moves rapidly, and so it is difficult to pick out everyone, but there at the foot of the grand staircase is Mr Andrews, who smiles at Rose with the happiest and warmest of smiles. The camera pauses but a moment to take him in before it races up the staircase.

And there at the landing, of course, at the foot of the clock (set at that fateful moment of the sinking, 2:20), is Jack, and as he turns with a broad grin to face the camera, there is a cut, finally, to a different angle, so that now we not only see Jack and all the assembled ghosts, but also Rose herself. She is seventeen again, beautiful, strong and vibrant. She bounds

toward him, her breast heaving, her hair flowing, her long satin dress gliding over the steps. Jack takes her in his arms, and as they kiss, the crowd cheers.

The camera swings upward to the white oval skylight, and the screen itself turns white.

Notes

My thanks to my intrepid readers Charlie Bassett, David Crane, Betsy Loyd, Libby Lubin, Alex Nemerov, Steve Rachman, Phil Smith and Rob White. I also wish to thank Colby College and Wake Forest University for their generous grants that assisted me in the writing and publishing of this book.

1 Pierre Bourdieu, *Distinction*, trans. Richard Nice (Cambridge, Mass.: Harvard University Press, 1984).

2 Humorist Dave Barry envisions a sequel to Cameron's film, *Titanic II*, in which an evil villain with a gun prevents Jack and Rose from helping women and children into lifeboats. 'VILLAIN: Out of the way! I'm taking this lifeboat all for myself! JACK: It's Kenneth Turan, film critic for the Los Angeles Times! TURAN: That's right, and I shall stop at nothing to get off this ship, because the dialogue is terrible! JACK: Is not! TURAN: Is too!', 'A Titanic Splash (Again)', *Miami Herald*, 31 May 1998.

3 Kenneth Turan, 'Oscars '98: You Try to Stop It', *Los Angeles Times*, 21 March 1998, p. F1.

4 José Arroyo, 'Massive Attack', *Sight and Sound* vol. 8 no. 2 (NS), February 1998, p. 19.

5 Laura Miller, review, *Sight and Sound* vol. 8 no. 2 (NS), February 1998, p. 52.

6 David Ansen, 'Our Titanic Love Affair', *Newsweek* vol. 131 no. 8, 23 February 1998, p. 61.

7 Ibid., pp. 61–2.

8 Cartoon by Jack Ziegler, *Time*, 4 May 1998, p. 55. For a scholarly assessment, see Peter Krämer, 'Women First: "Titanic" (1997), Action-adventure Films and Hollywood's Female audience', *Historical Journal of Film, Radio and Television* vol. 18 no. 4, October 1998, pp. 599–688.

9 Ansen, 'Our Titanic Love Affair', pp. 60–1; Associated Press, 'Italian 12-year-old Goes to See Titanic Every Day', 13 March 1998; *Sugar* vol. 44, June 1998, p. 13.

10 Associated Press, 'Woman Dies Imitating "Titanic" Movie Scene', *International Herald Tribune*, 13–14 June 1998, p. 4; 'Ship Passengers Mimic "Titanic" Bow-Climb Stunt', *Buffalo News*, 19 May 1998, p. 4A, and '"Titanic" Imitators Told to Stay Off Bow Railing', *St. Petersburg (Florida) Times*, 7 June 1998, p. 9E. A year later, when the luxury liner *Sun Vista* sank near Malaysia, rescued passengers told of singing *Titanic*'s popular theme song, 'My Heart Will Go On', to buoy their spirits, and the captain explained that the evacuation of more than a thousand people into lifeboats had gone smoothly because he had previously shown his crew *Titanic* as part of their training. See 'On Sinking Ship, Scenes from "Titanic"', *New York Times*, 22 May 1999, p. A3; 'Cruise Ship's Officials Defend Delay', *Gazette* (Montreal), 24 May 1999, p.A3.

11 A satirical on-line newspaper from Madison, Wisconsin, *The Onion*, presents a faux front page for a faux 1912 news extra announcing *Titanic*'s sinking: 'WORLD'S LARGEST METAPHOR HITS ICE-BERG' shouts the banner headline. Beneath it in smaller caps: 'Titanic, Representation of Man's Hubris, Sinks in North Atlantic' and '1,500 Dead in Symbolic Tragedy'. According to *The Onion*, the following message was telegraphed from the rescue ship *Carpathia*: 'TITANIC STRUCK BY REPRESENTATION OF NATURE'S SUPREMACY STOP INSUFFICIENT LIFEBOATS DUE TO POMPOUS CERTAINTY IN MAN'S INFALLIBILITY STOP MICROCOSM OF LARGER SOCIETY STOP', Scott Dikkers (ed.), *Our Dumb Century: 100 Years of Headlines*

From America's Finest News Source (New York: Three Rivers Press, 1999), p. 13.

12 Conrad's essay, Hardy's poem and a wealth of other literary responses to the saga of the *Titanic* are astutely analysed in Jeremy Hawthorn's *Cunning Passages: New Historicism, Cultural Materialism and Marxism in the Contemporary Literary Debate* (London: Arnold, 1996), pp. 87–157.

13 Steven Biel, *Titanica: The Disaster of the Century in Poetry, Song, and Prose* (New York: Norton, 1998), pp. 41, 59, 53.

14 Quoted in Steven Biel, *Down with the Old Canoe: A Cultural History of the Titanic Disaster* (New York: Norton, 1996), p. 30. See also Wyn Craig Wade, *Titanic: End of a Dream* (New York: Rawson, Wade Publishers, 1979), pp. 64–5 and 291–4. Wade's book examines the public responses to the sinking and includes a detailed account of the official investigations in the aftermath of the disaster to determine what had gone wrong.

15 Quoted in Biel, *Down with the Old Canoe*, pp. 123–4.

16 See Ibid., pp. 123–4, 115 (and on other African-American reactions to the sinking, pp. 107–17). Biel, *Titanica*, pp. 89–90, provides the complete text of Leadbelly's 'The Titanic'; pp. 104–5 reprints 'The Floating Cemetery: A Conversation Among the Drowned Ones of the Titanic' from the *Jewish Daily Forward*, 28 April 1912. Wade, *Titanic*, p. 294, claims that the sinking of the *Titanic* stirred the enthusiasm of inner-city blacks:

> Just as black heavyweight Jack Johnson had recently trounced the 'Great White Hope' in the person of Jim Jeffries, so had inexorable fate sent the white man's 'practically unsinkable' ship to the bottom of the sea. Symbolically, the millionaires' lily-white liner was Jeffries on a colossal scale: The Anglo-American Dream had gone down far more dramatically than the Great White Hope, revealing the myth of white superiority and its fallible epicenter, technology, in the most blatant and embarrassing way imaginable.

17 The annotated script for *Titanic* exhaustively details and explains changes made by Cameron in pre- and post-production. See James Cameron, *Titanic: James Cameron's Illustrated Screenplay*, annotated by Randall Frakes with interview of Cameron by Frakes (New York: HarperPerennial, 1998). For other detailed accounts of *Titanic*'s pre-production and filming see Ed W. Marsh, *James Cameron's Titanic*, photographs by Douglas Kirkland (New York: HarperPerennial, 1997), and Paula Parisi, *Titanic and the Making of James Cameron* (New York: Newmarket Press, 1998). See also Stephen J. Spignesi, *The Complete Titanic* (Secaucus, New Jersey: Birch Lane Press, 1988), for discussion of the film's production and reception, including a section (pp. 337–44) on its various inconsistencies, inaccuracies and anachronisms.

18 See François Truffaut, *Hitchcock*, with collaboration of Helen G. Scott (rev. edn.; New York: Simon and Schuster, 1983), p. 138.

19 Old Rose's gesture parallels the moment in *Harold and Maude* (1971) when Maude, the free-spirited octogenarian, chucks a diamond engagement ring into the sea rather than allow her love for the youth who gave it to her to be debased by a costly material object, regardless of its sentimental associations.

20 Cameron, *Titanic*, p. 6, has identified Beatrice Wood (1893–1998) as the basis for Rose. Bred for a life in high society, Wood ran away from her domineering mother at the age of seventeen to pursue her independence. Joining avant-garde circles, she lived a bohemian life and was romantically involved with Marcel Duchamp. Subsequently dubbed 'the Mama of Dada', she became a ceramicist based in Ojai, California. See her autobiography, *I Shock Myself*, (rev. edn.; San

Francisco: Chronicle Books, 1988), and Michael Kimmelman's obituary tribute, 'A "Titanic" Figure of the Avant-Garde', *New York Times Magazine* (3 January 1999), p. 42.

21 Stephen Crane, 'The Blue Hotel', in Pascal Covici, Jr. (ed.), *The Red Badge of Courage and Other Stories* (New York: Penguin, 1991), p. 314.

22 R. W. B. Lewis, *The American Adam: Innocence, Tragedy, and Tradition in the Nineteenth-Century* (Chicago: University of Chicago Press, 1955). Jack's 'King of the World' declamation from the bow of the ship also calls to mind the apocalyptic finale of Raoul Walsh's *White Heat* (1949). There, the psychotic criminal Cody Jarrett (James Cagney) – in many ways the antitype to, if not also logical extension of, the American Adam – takes a last stand against the law from a position hundreds of feet in the air atop a huge oil-refinery tank. As he blows himself to Kingdom Come, he whoops with demented glee to his dead and equally psychotic mother, 'Made it, Ma. Top of the world.'

23 When *Titanic* was test-marketed at a sneak preview in the Minneapolis Mall of America, the learning-to-spit scene proved to be a favourite of the survey audience. Reports Paula Parisi:

> The studio had begged [Cameron] to cut the spitting scene; so had his fellow producers. Everyone thought it was gross. The actors didn't respond well to the written scene and said they'd feel uncomfortable acting it. But he liked it. … The spitting scene stayed, and when filming began, the actors actually enjoyed it. Now viewers were loving it. (Parisi, *Titanic* p. 191).

In *Rudeness & Civility: Manners in Nineteenth-Century Urban America* (New York: Hill and Wang, 1990), John F. Kasson argues that the embracing or rejection of 'good' manners has long been a way for Americans to position themselves politically. Kasson contends that 'established codes of behavior have often served in unacknowledged ways as checks against a fully democratic order and in support of special interests, institutions of privilege, and structures of domination' (p. 3). The spitting scene in *Titanic* and the varied responses to it by critics and general audiences attest to the continuing cultural and political significance of vulgarity and 'bad' manners.

24 Andrea S. Walsh, 'The Women's Film', in Gary Crowdus (ed.), *The Political Companion to American Film* (Chicago: Lakeview Press, 1994), p. 485.

25 Robert Henri, 'Individuality and Freedom in Art' (1909), in *The Art Spirit*, compiled by Margery A. Ryerson (1923); (New York: Harper & Row, 1984), p. 141.

26 Henry James, 'The Art of Fiction' (1888), in Leon Edel (ed.), *Selected Fiction* (New York: Dutton, 1953), p. 595.

27 Joseph J. Kwiat, 'Robert Henri and the Emerson–Whitman Tradition', *Publication of the Modern Language Association* vol. 71, part 1, September 1956, pp. 617–36.

28 'The Titanic Tragedy', *Appeal to Reason* (Girard, Kansas), 4 May 1912, p. 4, reprinted in Biel, *Titanica*, p. 95.

29 Wade, *Titanic*, p. 61.

30 'The Titanic Tragedy', in Biel, *Titanica*, p. 94.

31 '[Winslet's] beauty is accessible, not intimidating; women can feel themselves inside her skin,' Karen Schoemer explains in her discussion of *Titanic*'s appeal to female viewers, 'A Woman's Liberation', *Newsweek*, 23 February 1998, p. 64. According to Joan Jacobs Brumberg, *The Body Project: An Intimate History of American Girls* (New York: Vintage, 1997), p. 99, 'In the 1920s, for the first time, teenage girls made systematic efforts to lower their weight by food restriction and exercise.' The numerous illustrations and photographs compiled in the insert section of Brumberg's book (following p. 94) testify to changing ideals of adolescent female beauty in America over the past century.

32 Mark Twain, 'How to Tell a Story' (1895), in Walter Blair (ed.), *Selected Shorter Writings* (Boston: Houghton Mifflin, 1962), p. 242.

33 John Bowe, 'The Rip-Off Artist: Did Director James Cameron Steal Famous Photographs?', *New York*, 1 June 1998, p. 17.

34 Walter Benjamin, 'Theses on the Philosophy of History' (1940), in Hannah Arendt (ed.), *Illuminations*, trans. Harry Zohn (New York: Harcourt, Brace & World, 1968), p. 261.

35 Henry Adams to Anne Palmer Fell, 18 April 1912. Quoted in Biel, *Down with the Old Canoe*, p. 4.

36 I have never been a woman's rights man. I have always claimed that a woman could get her rights – man's, too – and if there is anything left she can get that, too, if she knows how to go about it. When everything else fails she has her persuasive powers that make the miser buy her sealskin coats, diamonds and fancy hats. I suggest, henceforth, when a woman talks woman's rights, she be answered with the word Titanic, nothing more – just Titanic. W. C. Rickster, 'A Man's View', Letter to the Editor, *St. Louis Post-Dispatch*, 26 April 1912, p. 14. Reprinted in Biel, *Titanica*, p. 143.

37 Hawthorn, *Cunning Passages*, pp. 109–25, quotes the poem in full and provides a detailed gender analysis.

38 Cameron interview with Randall Frakes in Cameron, *Titanic*, p. xiv.

39 Robert Hughes, *The Shock of the New* (New York: Knopf, 1981).

40 James Cameron (1988), quoted in Jonathan Law (ed.), *Brewer's Cinema: A Phrase and Fable Dictionary* (London: Cassell, 1995), p. 92. The phrase 'frenzy of the visible' is used by Linda Williams in accounting for the primitive and ritualistic power of pornographic cinema but it applies equally well, I think, to the action cinema. Williams, *Hardcore: Power, Pleasure, and the 'Frenzy of the Visible'* (Berkeley and Los Angeles: University of California Press, 1989).

41 A good introduction to both the sexual radicalism of the era and the conservative reaction to it is John D'Emilio and Estelle B. Freedman, *Intimate Matters: A History of Sexuality in America* (New York: Harper & Row, 1988), part III, 'Toward a New Sexual Order, 1880-1930'. On the changing mores of youth during this period, see Paula S. Fass, *The Damned and the Beautiful: American Youth in the 1920s* (New York: Oxford University Press, 1979). See also Pamela S. Haag, 'In Search of "The Real Thing": Ideologies of Love, Modern Romance, and Women's Sexual Subjectivity in the United States, 1920–1940', in John C. Fout and Maura Shaw Tontillo (eds), *American Sexual Politics: Sex, Gender, and Race Since the Civil War* (Chicago: University of Chicago Press, 1993), pp. 161–91, and Ellen Kay Trimberger, 'Feminism, Men, and Modern Love: Greenwich Village, 1900–1925', in Ann Snitow, Christine Stansell, and Sharon Thompson (eds), *Powers of Desire: The Politics of Sexuality* (New York: Monthly Review Press, 1983), pp. 131–52. Important considerations of 'alternative morality' authored at the time include Floyd Dell, *Women as World Builders: Studies in Modern Feminism* (1913) and *Love in Greenwich Village* (1926), Freda Kirchway; (ed.), *Our Changing Morality: A Symposium* (1924), and Margaret Sanger, *Woman and the New Race* (1920). See also Wood, *I Shock Myself*. Speaking for the generation that Beatrice Wood belonged to and Rose would have been part of, Sanger, p.117, writes, 'The need of women's lives is not repression, but the greatest possible expression and fulfilment of their desires upon the highest possible plane. They cannot reach higher planes through ignorance and compulsion. They can attain them only through knowledge and cultivation of a higher, happier attitude towards sex.'

42 See Christopher Heard, *Dreaming Aloud: The Life and Films of James Cameron* (Toronto: Doubleday Canada, 1997), p. 175.

43 Ibid., pp. 9–10.

44 Ibid., p. 6.

45 Gilbert Adair, *Flickers: An Illustrated Celebration of 100 Years of Cinema* (London: Faber and Faber, 1995), p. 36.

46 The tidal wave has a personal resonance for Cameron: 'It's been a nightmare of mine throughout my entire life, a vast wave rolling towards the shore, miles high, turning day into night. That dream, in my subconscious, became inextricably interwoven with the dread of death, and the specific dread of nuclear holocaust.' Quoted in Heard, *Dreaming Aloud*, p. 144.

47 Michael Tanner, *Wagner* (London: Flamingo, 1997), p. 154.

48 Music by James Horner, lyrics by Will Jennings, performed by Celine Dion. The *Titanic* soundtrack itself captured number 1 on the Billboard Hot 200 albums chart for 10 consecutive weeks and, within 17 weeks of release, had sold more than 17 million copies worldwide, making it the best-selling soundtrack recording in film history. See Parisi, *Titanic*, p. 222, also pp. 163–6 and 193–6; and Spignesi, *The Complete Titanic*, pp. 344–7.

49 Walter Isaacson, '"The Heart Wants What It Wants"', *Time*, 31 August 1992, p. 61. Allen's remark echoes the Counter-Enlightenment sentiment of seventeenth-century French cleric Bossuet, 'The heart has reasons that reason does not understand.'

50 John F. Kasson, *Amusing the Million: Coney Island at the Turn of the Century* (New York: Hill and Wang, 1978), provides numerous insights relevant to both the ship *Titanic* (an embodiment of what Kasson calls 'the technological sublime') and the mass-culture origins of the film *Titanic*.

51 Frederic Thompson (1907), quoted in Kasson, *Amusing the Million*, p. 66.

52 In Luna Park, 'the "Helter Skelter" or "Human Toboggan" was essentially a slide for adults. Participants rode an escalator to the top of a huge chute made of rattan, then rapidly coasted down its sinuous course, landing at the end on a mattress – all to the amusement of the onlooking crowd.' Kasson, *Amusing the Million*, p. 78.

53 Beatrice Wood, the hundred-year-old-plus bohemian potter upon whom Cameron based Rose, writes in her autobiography of a memorable summer evening in 1917:

> One night Marcel [Duchamp] and [Francis] Picabia took me to Coney Island. Because I feared roller coasters, they made me go on the most dangerous one over and over, until I could control my screams. They enjoyed themselves enormously. So did I, for with Marcel's arm around me, I would have gone on any ride into hell, with the same heroic abandon as Japanese lovers standing on the rim of volcanoes ready to take the suicide leap. (Wood, *I Shock Myself*, p. 37).

See also Kathy Peiss, *Cheap Amusements: Working Women and Leisure in Turn-of-the-Century New York* (Philadelphia: Temple University Press, 1986), ch. 5, 'The Coney Island Excursion'.

54 Stephen Crane, 'The Open Boat', in *The Red Badge of Courage and Other Stories,* p. 246.

55 Kasson, *Amusing the Million*, p. 72.

56 Walt Whitman, 'O Captain! My Captain' (1865–66), in Mark Van Doren (ed.), *The Portable Walt Whitman* (New York: Penguin, 1977), p. 243.

57 *The Watchtower*, magazine of the Jehovah's Witnesses, vol. 119 no. 7, 1 April 1998 ('Average Printing Each Issue: 22,103,000 … Now Published in 128 Languages').

Credits

TITANIC

USA
1997

Director
James Cameron
Producers
James Cameron
Jon Landau
Screenplay
James Cameron
Director of Photography
Russell Carpenter
Editors
Conrad Buff
James Cameron
Richard A. Harris
Production Designer
Peter Lamont
Music Composer/Score Orchestrations
James Horner

©Twentieth Century Fox Film Corporation and Paramount Pictures Corporation
Production Companies
Twentieth Century Fox and Paramount Pictures present
A Lightstorm Entertainment production
A James Cameron film
Executive Producer
Rae Sanchini
Co-producers
Al Giddings
Grant Hill
Sharon Mann
Associate Producer
Pamela Easley Harris

Production Executive
Louis G. Friedman
Lightstorm Productions
Al Rives
Mike Trainotti
Production Associate
Geoff Burdick
Production Supervisors
Gig Rackauskas
Additional:
Michael Levine
Escondido Tank Shoot:
Dana Belcastro
Key Production Co-ordinator
Stacy Plavoukos
Production Co-ordinators
Belinda Uriegas
LA:
Eve Honthaner
Halifax Contemporary Shoot:
Karla Morash
Set Co-ordinator
Rafael Cuervo
Unit Production Managers
Grant Hill
Anna Roth
Sharon Mann
Jon Landau
Unit Manager
Kevin Delanoy
Location Managers
Nicole Kolin
Halifax Contemporary Shoot:
Andrew McInnes
Post-production

Supervisor:
Lisa Ann Dennis
Controller:
Paula Catania
Production Consultant
Marty Katz
2nd Unit Director
Steven Quale
Assistant Directors
1st:
Josh McLaglen
2nd:
Sebastian Silva
Kathleen 'Bo' Bobak
Joaquin Silva
3rd:
Giselle Gurza
Key 2nd:
Jacinta Hayne
2nd 2nd:
A. Hugo Gutierrez Cuellar
Additional 1st:
Toby Pease
Additional:
T.C. Badalato
2nd Unit 1st:
Jonathan Southard
Halifax Contemporary Shoot
2nd:
Kristy Sills
Halifax Contemporary Shoot
2nd 2nd:
Mandy Ketcheson
Halifax Contemporary Shoot
3rd:
Craig Cameron
Script Supervisors
Shelley Crawford
2nd Unit:
Bertha Medina

Casting
Mali Finn
Associates:
Emily Schweber
Magui Jimenez
Rodolfo 'Rudy' Joffroy
Gemma Joffroy
Jesus Ignacio Santana
London:
Suzanne Crowley
Gilly Poole
Directors of Photography
Halifax Contemporary
Shoot:
Caleb Deschanel
Titanic Deep Dive:
James Cameron
2nd Unit Directors of Photography
Roy Unger
Aaron E. Schneider
2nd Unit Photographer
John Stephens
Camera Operator
Jim Muro
B Camera Operators
Guillermo 'Memo' Rosas
Halifax Contemporary
Shoot:
Harald Ortenburger
Steadicam
Jim Muro
Wescam Operators
Kurt Soderling
Halifax Contemporary
Shoot:
Steve Koster
Gaffer
John Buckley

Documentary
Director:
Ed W. Marsh
Director of Photography:
Anders Falk
Titanic Deep Dive
Technology Supervisor:
Michael Cameron
Lead Design Engineer:
Vince Catlin
Production Co-ordinator:
Anthony Allegre
Technology Co-ordinator:
Ralph White
Senior Technician/ROV Pilot:
Jeffrey N. Ledda
Visual Effects
Supervisor:
Robert Legato
Producer:
Camille Cellucci
Editor:
Bryan Carroll
Steve R. Moore
Consultant:
John Bruno
Co-ordinator:
Blerime Topalli
Special Visual Effects/ Digital Animation
Digital Domain
Visual Effects Producer:
Crystal Dowd
Digital Effects Supervisors:
Mark Lasoff
Judith Crow
Visual Effects Director of Photography:
Erik Nash
Visual Effects Line Producer:
Cari Thomas

Digital Compositing
Supervisors:
Michael Kanfer
Mark Forker
Digital Effects Producer:
Karen M. Murphy
Compositing Consultant:
Price Pethel
Lead Compositors:
Rick Dunn
Bryan Grill
Simon Haslett
Special Effects Co-ordinator:
Mark Noel
Character Integration
Supervisor:
Umesh Shukla
Data Integration Supervisor:
Matthew 'Teal' Butler
Motion Capture Supervisor:
André Bustanoby
Digital Stunt Sequence
Supervisors:
Mark Brown
Andy Jones
Digital Paraphernalia
Supervisor:
Kelly Port
Lead Morph Artist:
Christine Lo
Visual Effs Production
Manager:
Dean Wright
Model Supervisor:
Leslie Ekker
Key Compositors:
Claas Henke
Brent Prevatt
Scott Rader
Andrea Sholer
Animation Supervisor:

Daniel Robichaud
CG Technical Supervisor:
Bill Spitzak
Digital Ocean Supervisor:
Richard Kidd
Digital Ocean Artists:
John Gibson
David Isyomin
Nikos Kalaitzidis
Zsolt Krajcsik
Darren Poe
Sandor Rabb
Toshi Shiozawa
Paul Van Camp
Character Supervisor:
Daniel Loeb
Character Modeller:
Shawna Olwen
Digital Ship Artists:
Frank Aalbers
Alan Chan
Karl Denham
Rusty Ippolito
Andy Lesniak
Peter Nye
Digital Ship Model Lead:
Fred Tepper
Visual Effects Editor:
Michael Backauskas
Model Crew Chiefs:
George Stevens
Gene Rizzardi
Night Compositing
Supervisor:
Carey Villegas
MIR Sequence Compositing
Supervisor:
Jammie Friday
Visual Effects Art Director:
Kenneth Mirman
Digital Ship Extension

Supervisor:
Richard A. Payne Jr
Motion Capture Animation:
Dan Ma
Michael Sanders
Digital Compositors:
Jeff Olm
Jonathan Egstad
David Stern
Paul Kirwin
Ron Shock
Charles Meredith
Craig Halperin
Dave Lockwood
John Sasaki
Dennis Davis
Mimi Abers
Marc Scott
Sonja Burchard
Treena Loria
Donovan Scott
Larry Butcher
Additional Photography:
Victor Abbene
Additional
Photography/Cam Operator:
John Paszkiewicz
Digital Matte Painters:
Peter Baustaedter
Charles Darby
Martha Mack
Visual Effects Production
Co-ordinator:
Susan Thurmond
Digital Effects Co-ordinators:
Lisa Harriman Scott
Lisa Spence Lissak
Laura McDermott
Mikella Kievman
Allyse Manoff
Melissa Darby

Motion Control Operators:
James Rider
Tim Conway
Rotoscope Artists:
Mike Frick
Tonia Young-Bilderbeck
Byron Werner
Model Makers:
Tom Nicolai
Alan Pilkington
Tom Woessner
Scott Lukowski
Don Mariano
Carolyn Daley
Dottie Starling
Lead Rotoscope Artist:
Howie Muzika
Location Manager:
Harry O'Connor
Additional Visual Effects
VIFX
Visual Effects Supervisor:
Richard Hollander
Visual Effects Producer:
Joyce Weisiger
CG Supervisors:
Cheryl Budgett
Edwin Rivera
Visual Effects Production
Manager:
Dan Foster
Digital Effects Production
Manager:
Gene Kozicki
Lead Inferno Artists:
Mark Felt
Chris Ryan
Lead 2D Compositors:
Sean McPherson
Mary Leitz
Inferno Artists:

Scott Bogunia
Walt Cameron
John Heller
Chris Howard
Sean Hyun-In Lee
Candace Lewis
Cesar Romero
Jon Tanimoto
Digital Artists:
Hunter Athey
Dennis Bennett
Rafael Colón
Gregory Ellwood
Kelly Fischer
Gloria J. Geary
Uel Hormann
Jennifer Howard
Christopher Ivins
Rimas Juchnevicius
Garrett Lam
James Do Young Lee
Liz Lord
Keith McCabe
Mike Roby
Marc Rubone
Rick Sander
Andrew Taylor
Jonathan Wood
Tsz 'Gee' Yeung
Cybele Sierra
Serkan Zelezele
David Gutman
Digital Rotoscoping:
Mike Lamb
Marian Rudnyk
David Sullivan
Antonio Torres
Chief Technologist:
Mark A. Brown
Model Shoot Producer:
Lee Berger

Script Supervisor:
Jane Slater
Director of Photography:
Dave Drzewiecki
Jim Weisiger
Production Manager:
Gary Nolin
Motion Control Operators:
Paul Johnson
Bill McGill
Digital Department
Manager:
Craig Newman
First Assistant Director:
Mark Oppenheimer
Physical Effects Co-
ordinator:
Ed Felix
Production Co-ordinator:
Alicia Powers
Additional Visual Effects
Industrial Light & Magic
Visual Effects Supervisor:
Dave Carson
Digital Effects Compositing
Supervisor:
Jon Alexander
Digital Effects Matchmover:
David Hanks
Visual Effects Producer:
Tom Kennedy
Digital Effects Artists:
Tim Alexander
Donald S. Butler
Jeff Doran
Craig Hammack
Marshall Richard Krasser
Visual Effects Editor:
Tim Eaton
Associate Visual Effects
Producer:

Heather Smith
Rotoscope Lead Artist:
Jack Mongovan
Rotoscope Artists:
Cathy M. Burrow
Susan Goldsmith
Scanning Supervisor:
Joshua Pines
Additional Visual Effects
Cinesite, Inc
Digital Visual Effects
Supervisor:
Jerry Pooler
Digital Visual Effects
Producer:
Aaron Dem
Digital Compositors:
Abra Grupp
Nicole Herr
Marcel Martinez
Cristin Pescosolido
Lisa Pollaro
Lisa Dackermann
Digital Artists:
Corinne Pooler
Mike Castillo
Hilery Johnson
Joe Dubbs
Mark Lewis
James Valentine
George Oliver
Editor:
Steve Mate
Rotoscope Supervisor:
Karen Klein
Digital Imaging Supervisor:
Bob Fernley
Digital Visual Effects Co-
ordinator:
Chris Del conte

Additional Visual Effects
Banned From The Ranch
Visual Effects Supervisor:
Van Ling
Digital Artist:
Jordan Harris
Visual Effects Editor:
Hitoshi Inoue
Composite Artists:
Yukiko Ishiwata
Brian Holden
Visual Effects Producer:
Casey Cannon
Visual Effects Co-ordinator:
Crystal Foth
Additional Visual Effects
POP Film & POP Animation
Digital Compositing
Supervisors:
Adam Howard
Ken Littleton
Digital Compositors:
Jennifer German
David Crawford
Candice Scott
CG Technical Supervisors:
Barry Robertson
Matt Hightower
Visual Effects Producer:
Andrea D'Amico
Computer Animators:
Kirk Cadrette
Som Shankar
Additional Visual Effects
4-Ward Productions
Visual Effects Supervisor:
Robert Skotak
Producer/Director of
Photography:
Mark Shelton

Production Co-ordinator:
Kathy Draper
Supervisor/Director of
Photography:
Dennis Skotak
Visual Effects Editor:
Bill Black
Executive Producer:
Elaine Edford
Model Maker:
Jim Davidson
Camera Operator:
Bryan Greenberg
Additional Visual Effects
CIS Hollywood
Visual Effects Supervisor:
Dr Ken Jones
Technical Supervisor:
Bill Feightner
Digital System Co-ordinator:
Bob Peishel
Senior Producer:
Joe Matza
Digital Compositing
Supervisor:
Jeff Heussler
Visual Effects Editor:
Dawn Llewellyn
Executive Producer:
C. Marie Davis
Digital Artists:
Danny Mudgett
Gregory Oehler
Suzanne Mitus-Uribe
Additional Visual Effects
Light Matters, Inc
Visual Effects Supervisor:
Mat Beck
Visual Effects Associate
Producer:
Chris Holt

3D Supervisor:
Colin Strause
Compositors:
Jodi Campanaro
Erik Liles
Compositing Supervisors:
Greg Strause
Edson Williams
Additional Visual Effects
Hammerhead Productions,
Inc
Jamie Dixon
Rebecca Marie
Thad Beier
Edie Paul
Additional Visual Effects
Matte World Digital
Visual Effects Supervisor:
Craig Barron
Chief Digital Matte Artist:
Chris Evans
Visual Effects Producer:
Krystyna Demkowicz
Digital Compositor:
Christopher Horvath
Additional Visual Effects
Pacific Title Digital
Digiscope
Perpetual Motion Pictures
Special Effects
Thomas L. Fisher
Co-ordinator:
Scott Fisher
Administrator:
Paula Fisher
Foremans:
Jay B. King
Sergio Jara Sr
Rigging Foreman:
Andrew Jesse Miller

Lifeboats/Large Scale Sinking Miniatures

Donald Pennington Inc

Frank Ayre

Mitch Bryan

Gary Young

Mike Wheelwright

Kathleen Myers

Chris Nakayama

Tom Gleason

Scott Alexander

Miles Clayton

Jon Craig

Mike Holdridge

Associate Editor

Roger Barton

Supervising Art Director

Charles Lee

Art Directors

Martin Laing

Additionals:

Neil Lamont

Bob Laing

Escondido Tank Shoot:

Bill Rea

Set Designers

Marco Niro

Dominic Masters

Peter Francis

Set Decorators

Michael Ford

Halifax Contemporary

Shoot:

Ali Rubenstein

Halifax Contemporary

Shoot:

Claude Roussel

Jason Shurko

Jack's Sketches

James Cameron

Scenic Artist

Steve Sallybanks

Storyboard Artists

Rick Newsome

Phil Keller

Eric Ramsey

Costume Designer

Deborah L. Scott

Men's Costume Supervisors

Adolfo Ramirez

Tom Numbers

Women's Costume Supervisor

Sarah Touaibi

Key Make-up

Artist:

Tina Earnshaw

Halifax Contemporary

Shoot:

Laura Borzelli

Make-up

Artists:

Sian Griegg

Polly Earnshaw

Enzo Mastrantonio

Rebecca Lafford

Lisa McDevitt

Additional:

Raul Sarmiento Pina

Debbie Gower

Mel Gibson

Toni Riki

Diyan Rogers

Teresa Patterson

Anita E. Brabec

Guadalupe Perez P.

Humberto Escamilla

Old Rose Special Effects Make-up

Greg Cannom

Key Hairdressers

Simon Thompson

Kay Georgiou

Key Hairstylist

Halifax Contemporary

Shoot:

Ann Townsend

Hairdressers

Betty Glasow

John Henry Gordon

Zoe Tahir

Titles/Opticals

Pacific Title

Instrumental Soloists

Simon Franglen

Tony Hinnigan

Ian Underwood

Randy Kerber

Eric Rigler

James Horner

Vocal Performances

Sissel

Titanic Orchestra

Music Performed by

I Salonisti

Violins:

Lorenz Hasler

Thomas Füri

Cello:

Ferenc Szedlak

Double Bass:

Béla Szedlák

Piano:

Werner Giger

Steerage Band Music Performed by

Gaelic Storm

Additional Orchestrations

Don Davis

Music Supervisor

Randy Gerston

Music Co-ordinators
Michal Lali Kagan
Amy Rosen
Supervising Music Editor
Jim Henrikson
Music Editor
Joe E. Rand
Scoring Engineer
Shawn Murphy
Historical Music
Consultant
John Altman
Soundtrack
"My Heart Will Go On" by
James Horner, Will Jennings,
performed by Celine Dion;
"Valse Septembre" by Felix
Godin, performed by I
Salonisti; "Sphinx" by
Francis Popy, performed by I
Salonisti; "Alexander's
Ragtime Band" by Irving
Berlin, performed by I
Salonisti; "Wedding Dance"
by Paul Lincke, performed
by I Salonisti; "Vision of
Salome" by Archibald Joyce,
performed by I Salonisti; "Oh
You Beautiful Doll" by
Seymour Brown, Nat D. Ayer,
arranged by William Ross;
"Come, Josephine, in My
Flying Machine" by Alfred
Bryan, Fred Fisher, arranged
by William Ross; "Nearer My
God to Thee" by Lowell
Mason, Sarah Adams,
arranged by Jonathan
Evans-Jones, performed by I
Salonisti

Choreography
Lynne Hockney
Sound Design
Christopher Boyes
Sound Mixers
Mark Ulano
Halifax Contemporary
Shoot:
Doug Ganton
Recordists
Cary Stratton
Ann Hadsell
Joan Chamberlain
Scott Jones
Darren Mcquade
Boom Operator
Donavan Dear
2nd:
Jimmy Osburn
Halifax Contemporary
Shoot:
Reynald Trudell
Re-recording Mixers
Gary Rydstrom
Tom Johnson
Gary Summers
Christopher Boyes
Lora Hirschberg
Re-recordists
Ronald G. Roumas
Scott Levy
Al Nelson
Mark Pendergraft
Supervising Sound Editor
Tom Bellfort
Dialogue Editors
Gwendolyn Yates Whittle
Claire Sanfilippo
J.H. Arrufat
Richard Quinn

Sound Effects Editors
Ethan Van der Ryn
Scott Guitteau
Christopher Scarabosio
ADR
Mixers:
Dean Drabin
Brian Ruberg
Tony Anscombe
Supervising Editor:
Hugh Waddell
Editors:
Suzanne Fox
Harriet Fidlow Winn
Richard G. Corwin
Cindy Marty
Lee Lemont
Foley
Artists:
Sarah Monat
Robin Harlan
Paramount Mixer:
Randy K. Singer
Supervising Editor:
Thomas Small
Editors:
Scott Curtis
Tammy Fearing
Dave Horton Jr
Aquatic
Supervisor/Researcher
Charlie Arneson
Marine Co-ordinators
Lance Julian
Halifax Contemporary
Shoot:
Richard Fraser
Titanic Visual Historian
Ken Marschall
Titanic Historian
Don Lynch

Naval Consultant
Kit Bonner
Etiquette Coach
Lynne Hockney
Stunt Co-ordinator
Simon Crane
Stunts
Steve Griffin
Joey Box
Sarah Franzl
David Cronnelly
Gary Powell
Tom Struthers
Laurie Crane
Sy Hollands
Steve Crawley
Jamie Edgell
Leo Stransky
Dimo Lipitkovsky
Dusan Hyska
Martin Hub
Alistair Sutherland
Paul Heasman
Paul Herbert
Gabor Piroch
Marc Cass
Pavel Cajzl
Bill Weston
Eunice Huthart
Ignacio Carreño Lopez
Jan Holícek
Jaroslav Psenicka
Klaus Jindrich
Pavel Kratky
Tim Trella
Cris Thomas-Palomino
Gabriela Moreno Flores
Kiran Shah
Mark Henson
Ray L. Nicholas
Sean McCabe

Andy Bennett
Dana Dru Evenson
Jani D. Davis
Jaroslav Peterka
Ricardo Cruz Moral
Alejandro De La Pena
Jamie Landau
Jorge Casares
Raul Lopez Arteaga
Ray De-Haan
Troy Gilbert
Gerardo Moreno Flores
Erik Stabenau
Jim Palmer
Robert Inch
Dane Farwell
John C. Meier
Terry Forrestal
Annie Ellis
Debby Lynn Ross
Jorge Luis Corzo
Lee Sheward
Nancy Lee Thurston
Richard Bradshaw
George Fisher
Nody-Arden
Chuck Hosack
Derek Lea
Gary L. Gurcio
Glenn Boswell
Johnny Hallyday
Leon Delaney
Vincent P. Deadrick Jr
Lawrence Woodward
Michael Papajohn
Johnny Martin
Lincoln Simonds
Glen Yrigoyen
Tim Rigby
Charlie Brewer
Mario Roberts

David Listvan
Gustavo Campos
Hernandez
Terry Jackson
Alfredo Gutierrez
Bernabe Palma
Wilebaldo Bucio
Lynn Salvatori
Mauricio Martinez Ramos
Paul Eliopoulos
Josh Kemble
Jill Brown
Lance Gilbert
Doc D. Charbonneau
Dustin J. Meier
Juan Manuel Vilchis Sosa
Julio Martĺnez
Simone Boisseree
Mark Dealessandro
Diane Peterson
Raleigh Wilson
Clarke Coleman
Clarke C. Coleman
Danny Rogers
John Casino
Justin Crowther
Terri Rippenkroeger
Jamie A. Keyser
Janet S. Brady
Debbie Lee Carrington
Kim K. Kahana Jr
Mic Rodgers
Mike Justus
Trisha Lane
Nancy L. Young
Rusty Hanson
Sandra Berumen
Victoria Vanderkloot
Anita Hart
Denise Lynne Roberts
Joni Avery

Julie Michaels
Matt Johnston
Rick Avery
Svetla Krasteva
Julie Lamm
Mike Avery
Steven Lambert
Cindy Folkerson
Kurt Lott
Larry Rippenkroeger
Marcia Holley
Bobby Andrew Burns
Johanna Mclaren-clark
Alejandro Avendaño Luhrs
Lisa Dempsey
Luis M. Gutiérez Santos
Lucy Allen
Paul Vokoun
Rafael Valdez Garcia Conde
Animal Trainers
Sled Reynolds
DeAnn Zarkowski
Elizabeth McMullen
Camera Helicopter Pilot
Halifax Contemporary
Shoot:
Chuck Tamburro

Cast
Leonardo DiCaprio
Jack Dawson
Kate Winslet
young Rose DeWitt Bukater
Billy Zane
Cal Hockley
Kathy Bates
Molly Brown
Frances Fisher
Ruth DeWitt Bukater
Bernard Hill
Captain Smith

Jonathan Hyde
Bruce Ismay
Danny Nucci
Fabrizio
David Warner
Spicer Lovejoy
Bill Paxton
Brock Lovett
Gloria Stuart
old Rose DeWitt Bukater
Victor Garber
Thomas Andrews
Suzy Amis
Lizzy Calvert
Lewis Abernathy
Lewis Bodine
Nicholas Cascone
Bobby Buell
Dr Anatoly M. Sagalevitch
Anatoly Milkailavich
Jason Barry
Tommy Ryan
Ewan Stewart
First Officer Murdoch
Ioan Gruffudd
Fifth Officer Lowe
Jonny Phillips
Second Officer Lightoller
Mark Lindsay Chapman
Chief Officer Wilde
Richard Graham
Quartermaster Rowe
Paul Brightwell
Quartermaster Hichens
Ron Donachie
master at arms
Eric Braeden
John Jacob Astor
Charlotte Chatton
Madeleine Astor

Bernard Fox
Colonel Archibald Gracie
Michael Ensign
Benjamin Guggenheim
Fannie Brett
Madame Aubert
Jenette Goldstein
Irish mommy
Camilla Overbye Roos
Helga Dahl
Linda Kerns
3rd class woman
Amy Gaipa
Trudy Bolt
Martin Jarvis
Sir Duff Gordon
Rosalind Ayres
Lady Duff Gordon
Rochelle Rose
Countess of Rothes
Jonathan Evans-Jones
Wallace Hartley
Brian Walsh
Irish man
Rocky Taylor
Bert Cartmell
Alexandre Owens
Cora Cartmell
Simon Crane
Fourth Officer Boxhall
Edward Fletcher
Sixth Officer Moody
Scott G. Anderson
Frederick Fleet
Martin East
Lookout Lee
Craig Kelly
Harold Bride
Gregory Cooke
Jack Phillips

Liam Tuohy
Chief Baker Joughin
James Lancaster
Father Byles
Elsa Raven
Ida Straus
Lew Palter
Isidor Straus
Reece P. Thompson III
Irish little boy
Laramie Landis
Irish little girl
Amber Waddell
Alison Waddell
Cal's crying girls
Mark Rafael Truitt
Yaley
John Walcutt
first class husband
Terry Forrestal
Chief Engineer Bell
Derek Lea
Leading Stoker Barrett
Richard Ashton
Carpenter John Hutchinson
Sean M. Nepita
elevator operator
Brendan Connolly
Scotland road steward
David Cronnelly
crewman
Garth Wilton
first class waiter
Martin Laing
promenade deck steward
Richard Fox
first steward
Nick Meaney
second steward
Kevin Owers
third steward

Mark Capri
fourth steward
Marc Cass
first hold steward
Paul Herbert
second hold steward
Emmett James
first class steward
Christopher Byrne
stairwell steward
Oliver Page
Steward Barnes
James Garrett
Titanic porter
Erik Holland
Olaf Dahl
Jari Kinnunen
Bjorn Gunderson
Anders Falk
Olaus Gunderson
Martin Hub
Slovakian father
Seth Adkins
Slovakian 3 year old boy
Barry Dennen
praying man
Vern Urich
man in water
Rebecca Jane Klingler
mother at stern
Tricia O'Neil
woman
Kathleen Dunn
woman in water
Romeo Francis
Syrian man
Mandana Marino
Syrian woman
Van Ling
Chinese man

Bjørn
Olaf
Dan Pettersson
Sven
Shay Duffin
pubkeeper
Greg Ellis
Carpathia steward
Diana Morgan
news reporter
I Salonisti
Titanic orchestra
Gaelic Storm
[Samantha Hunt
Stephen Twigger
Shep Lonsdale
Patrick Daniel Murphy
Stephen C. Wehmeyer]
steerage band
Kris Andersson
Bobbie Bates
Aaron James Cash
Anne Fletcher
Ed Forsyth
Andie Hicks
Scott Hislop
Stan Mazin
Lisa Ratzin
Julene Renee
dancers

[uncredited]
James Cameron
man at dance
Tony Kenny
deckhand
Don Lynch
Frederick Spedden
Francisco Váldez
man being combed for lice

[scenes deleted]
Adam Barker
Cyril Evans, SSCalifornian's
wireless operator

Dolby digital/SDDS/
Digital DTS sound
Colour by
CFI
Prints by
DeLuxe Laboratories
Anamorphic [Panavision]

filmed on location at Rosarita
Beach (Baja, California),
Vancouver (British
Columbia), Halifax (Nova
Scotia), Belmont Olympic
Pool (Long Beach,California)
and at the Titanic wreck in
the North Atlantic.

US Release Details
released on 19 December
1997
Distributor
Paramount Pictures
Certificate
PG-13
194 minutes 36 seconds
17,514 feet [35mm]

UK Release Details
released on 23 January 1998
[1st shown for the 51st Royal
Film Performance on 18
November 1997]

Distributor
20th Century Fox
Certificate
12
17,514 feet [35mm]
194 minutes 36 seconds

Credits compiled by BFI
Filmographic Unit

Also Published

L'Argent
Kent Jones (1999)

Blade Runner
Scott Bukatman (1997)

Blue Velvet
Michael Atkinson (1997)

Caravaggio
Leo Bersani & Ulysse Dutoit (1999)

Crash
Iain Sinclair (1999)

The Crying Game
Jane Giles (1997)

Don't Look Now
Mark Sanderson (1996)

Easy Rider
Lee Hill (1996)

The Exorcist
Mark Kermode (1997, 2nd edn 1998)

Independence Day
Michael Rogin (1998)

Last Tango in Paris
David Thompson (1998)

Once Upon a Time in America
Adrian Martin (1998)

Seven
Richard Dyer (1999)

The Terminator
Sean French (1996)

The Thing
Anne Billson (1997)

The 'Three Colours' Trilogy
Geoff Andrew (1998)

The Right Stuff
Tom Charity (1997)

The Wings of the Dove
Robin Wood (1999)

Women on the Verge of a Nervous Breakdown
Peter William Evans (1996)

WR – Mysteries of the Organism
Raymond Durgnat (1999)

Forthcoming

Dead Man
Jonathan Rosenbaum (2000)

Pulp Fiction
Dana Polan (2000)

Saló, or the Hundred and Twenty Days of Sodom
Gary Indiana (2000)

Thelma and Louise
Marita Sturken (2000)

1990s CINEMA FROM BFI MODERN CLASSICS

BFI MODERN CLASSICS
The Wings of the Dove
Robin Wood

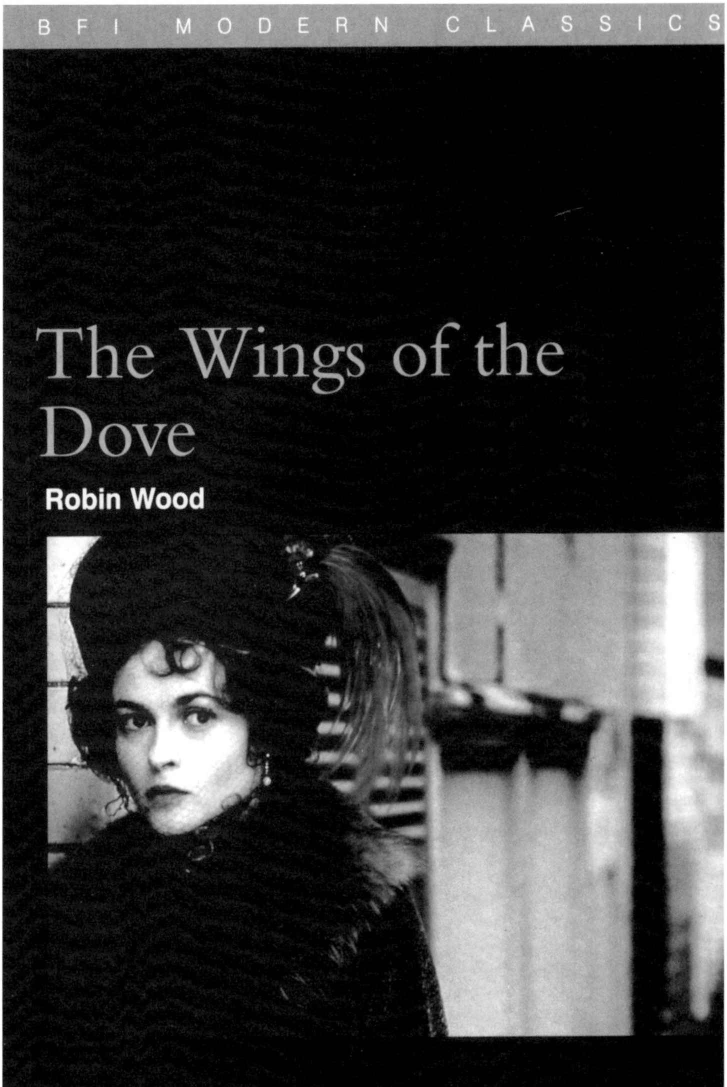

Crash

Iain Sinclair

BFI Modern Classics is an exciting new series which combines careful research with high quality writing about contemporary cinema. Authors write on a film of their choice, making the case for its elevation to the status of classic. The series will grow into an influential and authoritative commentary on all that is best in the cinema of our time.

If you would like to receive further information about future **BFI Modern Classics** or about other books on film, media and popular culture from BFI Publishing, please fill in your name and address and return this card to the BFI*.

No stamp needed if posted in the UK, Channel Islands, or Isle of Man.

NAME

_____

ADDRESS

_____

_____

POSTCODE

_____

* North America: Please return your card to:
Indiana University Press, Attn: LPB, 601 N Morton Street,
Bloomington, IN 47401-3797

**BFI Publishing
21 Stephen Street
FREEPOST 7
LONDON
W1E 4AN**